THE ECOLOGY OF FAITH

THE ECOLOGY
OF FAITH

By JOSEPH SITTLER

MUHLENBERG PRESS

PHILADELPHIA

Type used in this book
Body, 10 on 13 and 9 on 11 Janson
Display, Janson
Paper: Spring Grove Antique "RRR"

PREFACE

The occasion to write the material here presented was the invitation from the Yale Divinity School to deliver the Lyman Beecher Lectures on preaching in 1959. For the honor of that invitation, for the courteous attention of members of the faculty and students, and for useful critical reflections which I have tried to weigh I am grateful.

This little book is dedicated to my father. He was my first and best teacher. As I live and work and preach in a theological and general scene so different from that within which he served the church for over fifty years, I sometimes try to specify in my own mind the components of his still memorable sermons. The answer seems to be this: he lived with complete immediacy within the world of the Bible. He announced, administered, celebrated the gospel in preaching. The biblical images required from him no demythologizing; he intuitively understood them as Godly powers. The biblical words required no symbolization, for he never regarded them as anything but salvatory force. The stories in the Bible were not for him condensed moralizations from the long ago and far away. They were living transcripts of how a gracious God dealt and deals with his erring and unfaithful children.

The publisher and author record their grateful acknowledgment to the following houses for permission to quote from the items cited: Criterion Books, Inc., for George Barker's lines from *Elegy: Separation of Man from God;* Columbia University Press, *The Seventeenth Century Background;* J. M. Dent and Sons, Ltd., *Portable Conrad;* Dodd, Mead and Company, *Orthodoxy;* Harcourt, Brace and World, Inc., *The Complete Poems and Plays of T. S. Eliot;* Holt, Rinehart and Winston, Inc., *Complete Poems of A. E. Housman;* The Macmillan Company, *The Primacy of Faith;* G. P. Putnam's Sons, *The Art of Writing;* Random House, *The Collected Poetry of W. H. Auden;* Charles Scribner's Sons, *The Resurrection and Historical Reason;* The Bethany Press, *The Nature of the Unity We Seek.*

Permission to include the poems of Walter de la Mare has been granted by The Literary Trustees of Walter de la Mare and The Society of Authors as their representative.

TABLE OF CONTENTS

TO MY FATHER
WITH GRATITUDE AND AFFECTION

1

THE ECOLOGY OF FAITH, AND
THE NEW PREACHING SITUATION

It is now more than sixteen years since I was called away from a parish and a pulpit to assume the ministry of teaching. That fact is remembered here at the outset because it has determined the substance of these lectures. Lectures on preaching would normally and reasonably be assumed to have been prepared by a regular practitioner of the craft who, having actualized certain convictions about substance and method, has now undertaken to order and articulate his ideas.

That assumption in the present instance is not correct, and on several grounds. The elaboration of these may be a useful introduction to the following hours. During the years I have been a teacher of systematic theology I have continued to preach, most often in college and university chapels. Both foci of my work, that is to say, have been spheres of swirling change. As a teacher of theology one is exposed to and participates in the huge demolition and the tentative theological reconstruction of this twentieth century. As a university preacher one is obliged to declare the thus mauled but persistent message at the very place where the forces which make it difficult to communicate, to hear, and to apprehend, enjoy the most open field, inform the most esteemed disciplines, and have access to the most mobile minds.

I cannot, further, address you out of a confidence matured in almost thirty years of preaching. For I am steadily less confident of the adequacy of the ways I have gone for the time in which we now are, and am quite certain that they will not do in the years ahead. What has been done is not repudiated; it is simply assessed in terms of efficiency and communicative vitality, and found wanting in fresh circumstances. Forms of communication must change as one's mind 'and spirit grope toward larger meanings and as one sees the faces that look up at him to be eloquent with fresh problems, apprehensions, loves, hopes. In my city, as in yours, new forms of architecture are springing up to enclose new functions or to enclose old ones in a new way. It means something for every craftsman that these forms celebrate new materials and textures, that there seems to be a fresh delight in sheer cleanliness of line in this cluttered world, that forthright candor of statement is both proffered and received. A building by Mies van der Rohe is similar to the structure of a sentence by Ernest Hemingway. One cannot sermonically address men who produce and live in the steel and glass world of form in ways fashioned out of and for another time. Here, too, form follows function.

Now, therefore, I want to share with you some of the questions I ponder as I try to learn how to preach to my time, and certain ideas which I am weighing in the process of that endless work of obedience.

The first lecture, "The Ecology of Faith," is an effort to illuminate the present situation of preacher and parish by exploring the relational determinants suggested by the science of ecology. The second, "The Search For Theological Method, and Its Requirement of Preaching," is an inquiry into the central meaning of this search, and an effort to suggest how our practice in preaching may be changed by its occurrence. The third, "The Role of the Imagination in Preaching," is a kind of public payment of a debt! If I have learned anything about how to transform a theological assertion into an invitatory religious address, my constant teacher has been the Apostle to the Gentiles. The tight sequences of Paul's thought are not more characteristic than his amazing leaps; and in my own experiences as a preacher, the open space between the taking-off place and the landing place has been profoundly instructive. The fourth is a continuation of the third, an effort to reflect upon and reenact the delicate process whereby the mind and the imagination move from the place of hearing to the public celebration of the thing heard. The final lecture is but the articulation of a protest directed to those who alone can do anything about what I have called the "Maceration of the Minister." The substance of that lecture is less for the ears of the ministers than for those of the people in our parishes and for the executive officials in our general bodies. I say it in the context of these lectures on the legitimate ground that the macerated minister is operationally restrained from doing what the Lyman-Beecher lectures were intended to help him to do; and on the possibly illegitimate ground that this shout might be amplified from as prestigious a pulpit as is available for me.

Ecology is defined as the science that deals with the mutual relationship between organisms and their environment. As I have reflected upon the many elements that constitute the situation to which Christian preaching is directed I have sought for an analogy big enough and rich enough to do justice to all the trees, and at the same time lure the mind to the forest. The facts of the biological and botanical world seem to supply such an analogy.

On the bank of a river that flows between high hills is a village. It has been there for centuries. The village has made an arrangement with the vernal and autumnal moods of the river: the

houses and shops know how much the river rises with the spring
runoff of the snow water and with the fullness of the autumn
rains. Well up the bank they keep their distance. High in the
forest-covered hills, too, a right relationship exists between trees
and earth and forest animals and insects. By virtue of a mar-
velous ecological balance the life of each is regulated by the
function of the others. Under the bark of the trees, for instance,
there are millions of beetles which, undisturbed, would destroy
the trees. But they do not destroy the trees because beetles
are food for woodpeckers and the birds devour the beetles in
such numbers as to keep the margin safe. On any summer's day
in my part of the country one can hear the birds about their
happy ecological business! But one day a great beetle-infested
tree so falls upon the soft-mounded earth that its underside is
inaccessible to the birds. Thus protected, the beetles proliferate
in the rotting timber. They spread from tree to tree now in
such numbers that the bird-beetle balance is destroyed.

Tree after tree is attacked, invaded, killed. The first ravaged
acre increases to a dozen denuded hillsides. The billions of miles
of earth-gripping hair roots die. When the rains come and the
melting snow water gathers to a flood, the earth sponge, loosened
now, nonfibrous and helpless, pours the water down the slope
and with it the accumulated rich earth of unnumbered forest
seasons. The old rhythm of the river is broken by a process that
began with a strangely falling tree. The shops and houses at
the river bank are flooded in the spring because the beetles on
the far hills had an uninterrupted cycle of life.

Every situation in which the Word of God is declared in
preaching is a place and a moment on the riverbank; and the
permeability of that time and place to the declared Word is
bound up with the forests, the birds, the beetles, and the waters
of history. From Incarnation to culture is a straight line, for the
determination of God to embody his ultimate Word places man's

relation to that Word inextricably in the web of historical circumstances. The Word is not naked, it is historically embodied. The hearing situation is not naked either, and culture is the name for that ecological matrix in which the embodied will and deed from above addresses the embodied hearer at every point along history's river.

The depth, opulence, and vitality of a culture is determined by the fullness with which each episode in thought, feeling, and action is heavy with this ecological matrix. Men may think, feel, and act in ways that are novel, unprecedented, tradition-breaking and still preserve unbroken that power and content of the past whereby the life of culture is enriched. Hawthorne is deeply honored for his role in the articulation of the American character because he was creatively appreciative of what he repudiated and knew to be dead. And Joseph Conrad, a virtuoso among twentieth-century recorders of the demonic potential in the liberated life of the modern man, could write, ". . . for life to be full and large it must contain the care of the past and of the future in every passing moment of the present."

What is to be observed in that statement is the choice of the term *care* to designate the feeling-tone that pervades a man as he stands at the evanescent borderline between the "not yet" and the "no longer." Care is neither sentiment nor acquiescence; it suggests neither uncritical accumulation nor idealizing evaluation. To care is to cherish because a thing is given, because one has been there, because every field of dishonor or of praise is alive in the rich leaf mold of the unfolding years. This ecology of the spirit is what informs and sings out of memorable utterances which are hauntingly compounded of gallantry and pathos, memorable in virtue of evocative powers that escape analysis.

> Full fathom five thy father lies:
>   Of his bones are coral made;
>   Those are pearls that were his eyes;

> Nothing of him that doth fade
> But doth suffer a sea-change
> Into something rich and strange.[1]
>
> SHAKESPEARE

Or this, from a Cambridge lecture by Arthur Quiller-Couch:
"Is it possible, gentlemen, that you can have read one, two, three,
or more of the acknowledged masterpieces of English literature
without having it borne in on you that they are great because
they are alive, and traffic not with cold celestial certainties, but
with men's hopes, aspirations, doubts, loves, hates, breakings of
the heart; the glory and the vanity of human endeavor, the
transcience of beauty, the capricious uncertain lease on which
you and I hold life, the dark coast to which we inevitably steer;
all that amuses, or vexes, all that gladdens, saddens, maddens us
men and women on this brief and mutable traject which yet must
be home for a while, the anchorage of our hearts?"
Or this, in the quiet imagery of Walter de la Mare:

> Very old are the woods;
> And the buds that break
> Out of the briar's boughs,
> When March winds wake,
> So old with their beauty are—
> Oh, no man knows
> Through what wild centuries
> Roves back the rose.
>
> Very old are the brooks;
> And the rills that rise
> Where snows sleep cold beneath
> The azure skies
> Sing such a history
> Of come and gone,
> Their every drop is as wise
> As Solomon.

[1] Excerpt from "A Sea Dirge," in *The Tempest*.

> Very old are we men;
> Our dreams are tales
> Told in dim Eden
> By Eve's nightingales;
> We wake and whisper awhile,
> But, the day gone by,
> Silence and sleep like fields
> Of amaranth lie.[2]

Or, finally, this in the thought and austere lyricism of T. S. Eliot:

> Home is where one starts from. As we grow older
> The world becomes stranger, the pattern more complicated
> Of dead and living. Not the intense moment
> Isolated, with no before and after,
> But a lifetime burning in every moment
> And not the lifetime of one man only
> But of old stones that cannot be deciphered.[3]

The new preaching situation, were one exhaustively to catalog the elements that constitute it, would require a long essay. Attention would have to be given to issues of a biblical, historical, and theological kind which in their number and complexity torment the mind of the responsible preacher of the gospel. From Q to Qumran is one axis; and along it are strung the conclusions and constructions that every student knows by the names of Strauss, Ritschl, Herrmann, Harnack, Schweitzer, Dodd, and Bultmann. From Comte to Carnap is a second axis; and along it, troubling the mind with possibilities of basic error and exultant with hermeneutical possibilities for fresh articulation of kerygmatic eventful truth, are strung the philosophical, social, and linguistic analyses that every student knows by the names of Kierkegaard,

[2] Walter de la Mare, "All That's Past," *Collected Poems, 1901-1918* (New York: Henry Holt & Co., Inc., 1941), I, 128.

[3] T. S. Eliot, *The Complete Poems and Plays, 1909-1950* (New York: Harcourt Brace and World, Inc., 1952), p. 144.

Weber, Troeltsch, Dilthey, Marx, Freud, and the current practitioners of the meaning of meaning.

But we have been, let us assume, through all of that. These and other mentors have warned and instructed, demolished and rebuilt our understanding of the production and transmission of the biblical text, and have made us aware of the multitudinous forces that have thudded it into its received form. We are aware also of the career of this record in the history of the church, and of the oceans of ecclesiological, dogmatic, ethical, devotional, mystical discourse that have been engendered by analysis and contemplation of it. The sum of all of this is the substantial ecology of the faith of the Christian church at this moment—the moment when, with this record of the gospel of Jesus Christ before us, we stand up to preach.

In order to make concrete that preaching situation let us assume further that I am a preacher in a church which owns and honors the liturgical tradition, and as a major obedience to that tradition does not deliver over to me—for exploitation according to my ambulatory penchants or enthusiasms—a merely religious occasion, but has from of old designated this Sunday as the second Sunday in Advent. In most American Protestant parishes the old lectionaries are, to be sure, not followed; but to point that out has really nothing to do with the difficulty I want presently to expound. For these lectionaries include within their various sections—Gospel, Epistle, Introit, and Gradual—a large body of the most memorable and central addresses of the scriptures to the worshiping generations in the church. If one is not stuck with Luke 21:25-36 on the second Sunday of Advent he is not thereby released from the thundering New Testament words about the signs of the times, the invasive and convulsive power of the kingdom, the perils of drunkenness and stupidity in the midst of crises which are rich in threats of damnation and promises of redemption. And if one is not stuck with Rom. 15:4-13 on this

December Sunday, he can hardly avoid being stuck with it sometime—particularly since the sheer black hopelessness of men and the world cries aloud for some sober word; and even the churches at Evanston in 1954 affirmed that the Lord of the church *is* the hope of the world! The degree to which the waning authority of the lectionary has enabled the Protestant clergy to exercise so bland a selectivity within the corpus of New Testament utterances is a matter I observe but do not dilate upon.

It is, then, the second Sunday in Advent. As we attend now to what is being announced, affirmed, and pleaded for in the propers appointed for this day, have in mind the sheer magnitude of ecological richness and balance, the sheer allusive opulence which is presupposed as the matrix in which communication is ensconced. The Introit for the day is as follows: "Daughter of Zion: behold thy Salvation cometh. The Lord shall cause His glorious voice to be heard: and ye shall have gladness of heart. Give ear, O shepherd of Israel: Thou that leadest Joseph like a flock."

The tonality of the entire issue, and all the parts of it, is there resoundingly struck. The Gospel lesson is going to speak presently of the terrible "things that are coming on the earth" and of the new thing—". . . that the kingdom of heaven is nigh at hand." But men are called to in this fateful and choice-laden situation by no inert holiness ossified in his own perfections. Singing out in advance of the judgment, designating as love and pursuit the God with whom we have to do, soaring like a steady motif over all that is said of our situation in the Gospel, and grounding like a *continuo* the complex argument in the Epistle, come the infinitely tender words of the Introit. The Word of God is not thrown like a stone; rather is it, as Isaiah says, ". . . laid to the heart of Jerusalem." "Daughter of Zion: behold thy salvation cometh" as a father to a longed for child-daughter!

And as an active lover to his own city, wrought out over the covenant centuries for his glorious habitation. The fundamental nature of this seeking and salvation-bringing God and his historically authenticated resolution is lyrically acknowledged in the final line of the Introit, "Give Ear, O Shepherd of Israel: Thou that leadest Joseph like a flock."

It may be possible to announce that action of God in that kind of a relation to that kind of recalcitrance in nonallusive, propositional speech. And I am convinced, further, that the effort must be made. For the erosion that has gouged and gullied the fields of the vocabulary of faith is deep and impoverishing. And no man is ready to make an attack upon that problem who has not in sadness and clarity taken the measure of it. Let us not underestimate what is involved when we so easily assert that new ways must be found to make old affirmations! What precisely is involved is suggested in a section of a lecture, "On Reading the Bible," by Arthur Quiller-Couch:[4]

Although men do not go to the stake for the cadences, the phrases of our Authorized Version, it remains true that these cadences, these phrases, have for three hundred years exercised most powerful effect upon their emotions. They do so by association of ideas, by the accreted memories of our race enwrapping connotation around a word, a name—say the name *Jerusalem*, or the name *Sion*:

> "And they that wasted us, required of us mirth, saying,
> Sing to us one of the Songs of Sion.
> How shall we sing the Lord's song, in a strange land?
> If I forget thee, O Jerusalem, let my right hand forget her
>   cunning!"

It must be known to you, Gentlemen, that these words can affect men to tears who never connect them in thought with the actual geographical Jerusalem; who connect it in thought merely with a

[4] *On the Art of Reading* (New York: G. P. Putnam's Sons, 1920), pp. 145 f.

quite different native home from which they are exiles. Here and there some one man may feel a similar emotion over Landor's

> Tanagra, think not I forget . . . ,

But the word *Jerusalem* will strike twenty men twenty-fold more poignantly: for to each it names the city familiar in spirit to his parents when they knelt, and to their fathers before them: not only the city which was his nursery and yet lay just beyond the landscape seen from its window; its connotation includes not only what the word "Rome" has meant, and ever must mean, to thousands on thousands setting eyes for the first time on The City: but it holds, too, some hint of the new Jerusalem, the city of twelve gates before the vision of which St. John fell prone:

> Ah, my sweet home, Hierusalem,
>   Would God I were in thee
> Thy Gardens and thy gallant walks
>   Continually are green:
> There grows such sweet and pleasant flowers
>   As nowhere else are seen.
> Quite through the streets with pleasant sound
>   The flood of Life doth flow;
> Upon whose banks on every side
>   The wood of Life doth grow . . .

The process there so movingly described has gone on now for a long time, and its effects are general. But I want now to indicate three facts which I have encountered in my experience as a teacher, who, because he came to that function by way of the parish ministry, has never been able to have an immediate and lively sense of vocation save in relation to the church and its teaching and preaching obedience. Because, therefore, I see these three facts so deeply determinative among theological students in particular, but generally evident in this generation as a whole, I devote the remainder of this lecture to a description of them:

1) THE TYRANNY OF THE SELF

A long time ago St. Augustine affirmed that it was because of sin that man was deflected in his desire from his true end, the love of God, and ". . . curved inward upon himself . . ." perversely given to the self as an adequate end. Insofar as that is a true description of the general pattern of egocentricity that characterizes all men there is no great illumination in remarking that this generation is so disposed. What *is* new is that an incurvature which has traditionally been viewed in Christian pedagogy as a disposition to be overcome is among many in our day jubilantly cultivated as a way of redemption! There is a difference between regarding the self as a theatre of redemption and regarding the recovery of the self as the substance of redemption.

The term under which this absorption with the self is most commonly cultivated is existentialism. The historians of philosophical, theological, and literary existentialism will properly protest that the filching of the term by the self-absorbed is not only unwarranted but actually begets confusion. Soren Kierkegaard would certainly be astonished to know that his lifelong wrestling with God's angel was presently being interpreted in the categories of the personality sciences. St. Paul would certainly be astonished to hear the passionate inwardness of the vocabulary used to describe the relentlessness of God's Christly pursuit of man reduced to merely psychological categories.

The tyranny of which I am speaking is not lessened by niceties of designation. The reality of it is this: that we incline to define ourselves, take the measure of our actuality, admit as educative and civilizing, acknowledge as relevant and powerful—only that in experience or reflection which is authenticated by its occurrence within the biographical brackets of the self's existence. What is actually accomplished by this determination to admit as personal only what is authenticated as individual and inwardly certified is a radical reduction of the potencies for self-knowledge. For the self exists within an ecological matrix; and the address to, the description of, and the evangelical promises to the Christian self are embedded in that ecological web which is the faith of the Christian church. It is not necessary for the deepening and amplification of my understanding of what it means to become and be a Christian that I inwardly respond with incandescent recognition to every member of that "mighty cloud of witness" who, in the imagery of the letter to the Hebrews, surround and support my Christian race. It may in fact be a mighty gift to the self that it hear other selves in the stadium of the church catholic who make sounds of praise and joy which are as yet, and may remain, unattested within the cubicle of its own experience. One can acknowledge that he is unacquainted with what Paul meant when he said "I live, yet not I, but Christ lives in me", and at the same time have his individual existence broken open to fact by the assumption that the man knew what he was talking about, meant what he said, and lived out and died out the affirmation.

The extent to which men of this generation are absorbed with themselves and permit that absorption to filter the accumulated masses of human experience and utterance is a formidable fact in teaching and in preaching. In a course which I share with a colleague, a lecture was in progress dealing with pre-Chalcedonian alternatives to the statement there declared by the church. In the course of an exposition of the Nestorian position, justly illuminated with reference to strands in the New Testament witness to Christ which have made adoptionism an inevitable temptation, the lecturer was interrupted by the impatient protest of a student, "But Doc, I can't interiorize this stuff!'

This visceral authentication of the relevance of the history of doctrine would be merely humorous were it not symptomatic of something that is not humorous; and one could be patient with phases of development marked by fascinated picking away at the gossamer peculiarities of one's own insides if the damage wrought were not so extensive. The extent of that damage is apparent in much preaching of the gospel. Preaching becomes primarily personal, the history of the church becomes an anecdotal arsenal useful for its supply of supportive items. The "mighty deeds of God" are transformed into such interior "patterns of sensibility" as are readily marketable, and the mighty *TE DEUM* of the people of God becomes trivialized into a "worship experience."

2) THE TYRANNY OF BOUNDLESSNESS

When the theme of the second assembly of the World Council of Churches was announced, and more acutely when the preliminary study document was made available to the churches in North America, there was a curious reaction. The reaction was compounded of bafflement, annoyance, and impatience. Some were baffled by the declaration that nothing less than Jesus Christ was the hope of the world, for were there not broader, more generally "religious" and less radical sources for hope? Others were annoyed because they regarded this blunt statement as a frantic oversimplification of Christian theology, a retreat into pre-enlightenment piety. Others were impatient because they believed themselves allied with redemptive powers and possibilities whose adequacy was threatened by this identification of hope with so scandalous a historical particularity.

One does not take the measure of this reaction if he ascribes it merely to the fact that theological discourse in the United States has not had the role in intellectual life that characterizes European Christendom, or to the fact that we are a practical and activist people. There is that in our entire American experience on this continent which has deeply informed our self-consciousness. One might call it the mood of the illimitable. Frederick Jackson Turner, early in this century, inaugurated an epoch in

American historiography with his essay, *The Frontier in American History*. This historian affirmed that the particular quality of American historical thought and action was to be explained from the perspective of the frontier. His argument was impressive, and the implications of it have left untouched no enquiries into the American character.

In the following paragraphs an effort will be made to investigate whether and to what extent the mood of the boundless, so characteristic of the American spirit, constitutes a kind of soft and yielding tyranny into which the eschatological and bounded finalities of the gospel are absorbed without great effect. I have called this tyranny soft and yielding not by any means to suggest that it has not power and peril, but rather to pull into focus the kind of peril it is. A hard, tough, resistant surface is always more satisfying to fling the gospel at! There is impact and decisiveness in the thud of a ball against a brick wall. But to throw a ball into, let us say, a heap of cotton batting is an experience of quite another kind. The thing is unresistingly received, swallowed up, blandly absorbed as a part of the heap. And there is no thud. Is it possible to account for this mood, observe characteristic expressions of it, and assess what it means for our preaching?

Turner's essay called into question all the previous perspectives from which the events and the patterns of American life had been presented. These perspectives were generally oriented to the European continent, and hence saw the peculiar developments of American life and institutions in terms of unusual, to be sure, but continuous extensions of European life. American history was Colonial history. American politics was a marginal activity in European politics. American economic institutions were modifications of European institutions.[5]

[5] For discussion of this and other ideas in American historiology, see J. H. Randall and G. Haines, *Controlling Assumptions in the Practice of American Historians* (Social Science Research Council Bulletin 54 [1946]), p. 25.

This perspective does rough justice to wide areas of American life, and for a period of two hundred years or so after the first settlements it serves to make intelligible many activities on the new continent. But what was neither seen clearly nor enunciated precisely before Turner's essay was the deepening impropriety of this perspective as the nineteenth century unfolded. Such a perspective made sense of the Revolution of these colonies against Great Britain; it did not make sense of the Whisky Rebellion. This perspective was useful in doing justice to many aspects of the personal character and historical role of George Washington; it made less and less sense when confronted with the figures of Henry Clay, Andrew Jackson, and Ralph Waldo Emerson.

It is proposed here to speak of the development of the American self-consciousness in such terms as to take seriously Turner's thesis: that the blunt fact of the existence for many decades of a frontier in American history is a dominant factor in the content of America's self-consciousness. And inasmuch as any basic Christian affirmation is molded to the vital energies which work upon it in any nation or country, it ought to be possible to gain insight into the fact that classical Christian eschatology is interpreted in present American life in a peculiar way. This insight will be sought in the following enquiry.

The frontier was for many generations of Americans the symbol of the illimitable. For centuries before the white man established settlements in New England, at the mouth of the Hudson, in the Virginia Tidewater, and in the Carolinas, the living space of European peoples had been divided among the nations. These borders to be sure were in rather frequent flux and large movements of people were in process. But the space was a "given"! The North Sea, the Atlantic Ocean, the Mediterranean, were unrelenting borders. And to the east, the non-European peoples —Mongols, Huns, Turks, later the Russians—constituted an effective barrier. This barrier, indeed, was often penetrated, and

European literature from Marco Polo to Hakluyt shimmers with the mystery and possibility of these peoples and lands. But as regards its bearing upon the European spirit the East could not exercise effective force.

The situation in North America was completely and profoundly different. The early communities which hugged the Eastern shore lived their lives, did their work, and were subtly shaped in their thinking by the fact that what was settled was not what was available. Arching pervasively over the established situation was the knowledge that the West stretched out beyond like an illimitable sea. One has only to read the sermons of the early New England divines to remark how often and how eloquently this huge land, unknown in detail but known to be there, supplied illustrations for those passages in the sermon which required pictorial language to nail down a sermonic point.

The seemingly illimitability of the American land was not an isolated factor in the early American consciousness; it was a pervasive form of that consciousness. Our literature, the clearest confessional of our national self-consciousness, is permeated through and through with the mood of the vastness of the setting of the American enterprise. The journals of the Mathers, the Cottons, the Endicotts in New England, the travel diaries of Crevecoeur, the novels of James Fenimore Cooper and Herman Melville, the essays and public addresses of Ralph Waldo Emerson—all of these breathe an air which blows in from the open frontier. The very form of American humor in the nineteenth century is revealed by analysis to owe its vitality to this same situation. It is broad rather than witty, obvious and ribald rather than delicate and sly. It depends for its delight not upon the situations and ambiguities of the drawing room, the cultivated folk of the city, but upon the exaggerations, the trickeries, the buffooneries, and the fantastic human types so richly produced by the conventionless frontier. Mark Twain is America's artist of the ridiculous.

At a more sober and contemplative level one finds that American efforts to articulate the promise and hope of the young nation's role and place in history are informed by the language-shaping vastness of this illimitable land. Several instances will serve to illustrate how the breadth and the sweep of the midland prairies, the terrifying distances, the huge lakes and mighty rivers have imparted to the American dream a boldness of conception and an almost gargantuan excess of rhetoric.

About the middle of the nineteenth century Herman Melville, a New Yorker of Dutch descent, published his greatest novel. In the following passage it is not difficult to feel how the open illimitable frontier character of the American experience is taken as a clue to moral interpretation of man generally. It is a tribute to the power of this feeling that Melville—who almost alone among mid-nineteenth century men of letters in America pierced through the general moral optimism of the expansive spirit of the time, revealing in powerful fictional characters the ambiguities, the tensions, and the dark depths of evil and delusion — that *Melville* should have written these sentences. In them is the authentic note, later to come to full expression, that in the nascent American democracy was the solvent for man's immemorial problems, the answer to his whole dream of freedom and worth:

. . . it is a thing most sorrowful, nay shocking, to expose the fall of valor in the soul. Men may seem detestable as joint stock companies and nations; knaves, fools, and murderers there may be; men may have mean and meager faces; but man, in the ideal, is so noble and so sparkling, such a grand and glowing creature, that over any ignominious blemish in him all his fellows should run to throw their costliest robes. That immaculate manliness we feel within ourselves, so far within us that it remains intact though all the outer character seem gone, bleeds with keenest anguish at the spectacle of a valor-ruined man. Nor can piety itself, at such a shameful sight, completely stifle her upbraidings against the permitting stars. But this dignity I treat of is not the dignity of kings and robes but that abounding dignity which has no robed investiture. Thou shalt see it shining in the arm that wields a pick or drives a spike, that democratic dignity which, on all hands, radiates without end from God; Himself! The great God absolute! The center and circumference of all democracy! His omnipresence, our divine equality.[6]

Several decades later another Easterner, Walt Whitman, shattered the reigning forms of poetical expression and in a flood of tumultuous verse wrought out a voice for America's vague but deep and powerful feeling for her national character and promise. In his poetry, place names and common terms for common products of land and mine and forest are strung into melodious sequences that exercise the force of an incantation. The result is to produce—out of the sheer overwhelming rhythm of names that suggest space and scope, richness and distance—the intoxication of the illimitable. That this illimitable forward-leaning vitality foresees concrete achievements and conquests that are of doubtful moral significance is nothing to the point.

> Land of coal and iron! land of gold! land of cotton, sugar, rice!
> Land of wheat, beef, pork! land of wool and hemp! land of
> the apple and the grape!
> Land of the pastoral plains, the grass-fields of the world!
> Land of those sweet-air'd interminable plateaus!
> Expanding and swift, henceforth,
> Elements, breeds, adjustments, turbulent, quick and audacious,
> A world primal again, vistas of glory incessant and branching,
> A new race dominating previous ones and grander far, with new
> contests,
> New politics, new literatures and religions, new inventions and
> arts.[7]
>
> WALT WHITMAN

[6] Herman Melville, *Moby Dick* (New York: Alfred A. Knopf, Inc., 1930), p. 166.

[7] "Starting from Paumonok," *Leaves of Grass* (New York: Aventine Press, 1931), pp. 23 ff.

A second poem from Walt Whitman is instructive in this: that here the generality of the foregoing piece is given concreteness from the actual anecdotal record of the century of the winning of the West, and because there is revealed how the irremediable facts of limit, end, death are burned away in the sheer incandescence of the song of conquest and assertion.

> Come my tan-faced children,
> Follow well in order, get your weapons ready,
> Have you your pistols? have you your sharp-edged axes?
>> Pioneers! O Pioneers!
>
> Have the elder races halted!
> Do they droop and end their lesson, wearied over there
>> beyond the seas?
> We take up the task eternal, and the burden and the lesson,
>> Pioneers! O Pioneers!
>
> All the pulses of the world,
> Falling in they beat for us, with the Western movement beat
> Holding single or together, steady moving to the front, all for us.
>> Pioneers! O Pioneers!
>
> They are of us, they are with us,
> All for primal needed work, while the followers there in
>> embryo wait behind,
> We are today's procession heading, we the route for travel clearing,
>> Pioneers, O Pioneers![8]

WALT WHITMAN

In an introduction to a collection of lyrical passages from the novels of Thomas Wolfe, John Hall Wheelock compares him to Whitman, ". . . whose vision of America and the American continent he shared. The American spirit and the American earth of our day as distinguished from the spirit and earth of any other land or time, these are the major themes of Wolfe's writ-

---

[8] "Pioneers, O Pioneers!" *ibid.*, pp. 236 ff.

ing, and it is as a poet that he articulates them. In so doing he
has given many Americans a fresh sense of their country." [9]

This third writer who expresses the illimitable as a pervasive
and formative presence in the American mind is selected not only
for what he wrote but because of when he wrote it. Thomas
Wolfe was no frontiersman. He was born in North Carolina and
lived most of his life in the East; for the longest period of his
mature life in New York City. The following selection from
Wolfe is given here to advance the argument that the illimitable
as a mood of the mind persists within men who have never seen
a geographical frontier, and far beyond generations for whose
history it was a palpable fact. The fact of the frontier is not
gravely enough calculated if, as many historians have assumed,
the effect of it upon concrete political developments, forms of
community life, institutions, has been observed, measured, and
recorded. For the American man the frontier is a way of viewing
the human enterprise and a way of interpreting the life of the
traveler. It is a way of seeing long after it has something to see.
Writing of men in an old section of the South that he knew so
well Wolfe writes: "He is not a colonist, a settler, a transplanted
European; during his three centuries there in the wilderness he
has become native to the immense and lonely land that he inhab-
its; during those three centuries he has taken on the sinew and
the color of that earth, he has acquired a character, a tradition, a
history of his own . . . he is there in the ranks of the American
Revolution, and eighty years later he is there, gloriously but
silently in the ranks of the Civil War. But his real history is
much longer and much more extraordinary than could be indicated by these flares of war; it is a history that runs back three
centuries into primitive America, a strange and unfathomable

---

[9] Wheelock (ed.), *The Face of a Nation, Poetical passages from the
writing of Thomas Wolfe* (New York: Charles Scribner's Sons, 1939), p. v.

history that is touched by something dark and supernatural, and
that goes back through poverty and hardship, through solitude
and loneliness and death and unspeakable courage, into the
wilderness."

Another facet of this mood of the boundless is revealed when
one ponders the role of technology in modern American life.
Among us technology as a way of life is joyfully cultivated by
a people who retain a frontier mentality long after the physical
frontier has vanished. There is something strange in the joy and
eagerness with which the "technization" of existence is exercised
in America. This strangeness is understood when one comes to
see that the spirit that conquered a huge land is a spirit continuous with that which today plays with technics as a previous
generation made a game out of felling trees, shucking corn, and
plowing fields.

For the common man in America the basic physical enquiries
which gave birth to technology, and the philosophical ideas which
attended its development, are of little concern. Technology for
him is rather a stronger and a longer and a more supple arm to
conquer a wilderness with! His judgment of its "goodness" is
pragmatic; his delight in it is akin to sheer uncritical boyishness.
For in technology and its possibility to enhance and expand the
forms of life this man sees a new wilderness to conquer, new
lands to settle, new problems to solve, new frontiers to push
back and be exultant over.

That simple and uncritical acclaim should surround the advance of technology in America is evidence of the spirit that
has never had to come to terms with boundaries, limits, ends.
When one county was settled and the best land taken up, American history records that the new waves of people pushing up
from the East went through to the next county. There, when
once the trees were felled, the land cleared, was an abundance
of rich earth for man's taking. That land is now cut up into

organized states and most of it is settled. The farther ocean has been reached. But the promise of technology itself is seen in the American mind as a new "illimitable" that evokes from this people a response whose inward character is identical with the response of their fathers. A "new frontier" has come into view. and the excitement and the challenge of it is similarly greeted.

The entire experience of the peoples of America has created and nurtured a world view which stands over against the world view of the Bible in sharpest possible opposition. For "Eschatology is the doctrine concerned with the limits and boundaries of our living, in time and existence, toward which at every moment our whole lives tend." [10] In this statement is recollected a central affirmation of the scriptures that man's life, in solitude and in history, is found and held within the hand of God; that operating within history, and dramatically at the consummation of history, is the judging and restoring activity of history's God. There is a limit which stands not only at the end of human life as death, but which is built into the structure of human life by virtue of its creaturely character. All birth and development, all unfolding and enterprise, all moral vision and achievement are not only enfolded within this limit but receive their urgent character from it. Here is a "given" time, a "given" space, a "given" possibility. Within the boundaries of this "given" there are, to be sure, vast and absolutely crucial possibilities for affirmation or denial, hearing or deafness, decision or stasis—but no elaboration of these possibilities can avoid the limit of sin and of death.

The character of a people's life experience determines to some degree the permeability of their spirit to this Word. When the historical experience of the whole people is interpreted in such a way as to affirm the illimitable by virtue of an open frontier

[10] R. Calhoun, "Christ: The Hope of the World," published in the *official proceedings of the World Council of Churches, second assembly* (Evanston, Illinois: August 15, 1954).

existing for a long period of their history, then it surely follows that that declaration of the eschatological character of all existence will not easily address them with quick and intelligible meaning. Precisely this is the situation among millions of Americàns. For many of them a frontier situation has been transmuted from a fact of national history into a point of view in the mind. Only in recognition of the power of this inheritance can one understand the reception, bordering upon the charge of total irrelevance, with which many even within the churches regard the entire range of biblical eschatological teaching.

The eschatological reality becomes congruent with and partially confirmed in a man's life experience when absolute limits, boundaries, inescapable facts confront him in the realization of his personal, social, and national experience. These lessons can be evaded or their meaning dimmed when the "given" in practical experience is not absolute. When, for instance, as has been true for American generations, an intolerable, unsatisfactory, or restricting life situation began to press too hard, the frontier offered an escaping option. There has always been an "out there," an open, raw, malleable theater wherein patterns of desire dreamed of realization in forms nearer to the heart. To uproot the thousand continuities of one's life and settle in a wilderness required courage, decisiveness, resolution, ingenuity, and a huge output of activity. Hence the development of these qualities in the American national character. But in virtue of this same uprooting and transplanting career the occasion for the cultivation of another set of qualities has been successfully evaded. The realities of "limit" and "boundary," the spirit-educating forces that operate when one cannot move on, or start anew, but must come to terms with life where it is and where it is bound to remain —these forces have not deeply entered into the American national consciousness.

There are evidences, however, that the facts of America's new and responsible involvement in the revolutions, the agonies, the undeferrable decisions of the world is making her mind deepeningly permeable to the eschatological. Our debt to contemporary European scholarship in which biblical theological categories are freshly used as interpreters of the meaning of history is a large and growing debt. While, to be sure, the effect of such work is presently restricted to faculties and students in universities and schools of theology, the profound change in process will inevitably be projected in the preached and taught messages of the churches.

The question whether, short of concrete national tragedies, the frontier delusion of contemporary American can be translated into a realistic comprehension of man's bounded life, a strong and faithful obedience to God as he confronts us with hard tasks in the actual world where tyranny, brutality, aggressive nihilism is consolidating its bloody conquest, must await the evidence of the coming years.

3) THE TYRANNY OF OPAQUE LANGUAGE

By developing the various themes in this first lecture (indeed our entire discussion) under the large figure of Ecology a general intention is clearly stated: to argue that faith comes to exist in the vast and complex totality of a man's life, that faith as engendered by the Word of God works upon, makes use of, reillumines and reinterprets the total geography of existence. The proclamation of the Faith, and its transmission, must therefore operate within no narrower dimensions than the wild unsystematic of actual life. The theatre of redemption is the theatre of creation; anything has overt or covert influences upon everything; the beetles under the bark are the apprehension that furrows the brow that watches the untrapped waters destroy the town. Therefore I will discuss for a moment a third tyranny that characterizes the preaching situation.

Language, in its scope and style, takes on the color of the preoccupation of an age. If an age is marked by what one observer has called "the thingification of man" the speech of the age will both record what is happening and make articulate the cries of hurt wrung out of the monstrous process. For speech is the primary carrier of culture and its form follows man's career with an absolute seriousness. When grammar is sprung and words writhe, when images make leaps that baffle and astound, there is something other and something more wrong than can be ascribed merely to the disposition of the queer to be experimental.

People are round and have depth. And when their common language, used to do business in a technically preoccupied age, is shaped to the paucity of dimensions necessary to such business, the roundness and the depth become silent for want of verbal counterparts for the felt but inchoate self. Technical speech is a very efficient instrument. It is designative, precise, singular, flat, non-allusive; naming a certain device a cathode ray occilograph tells the company of operators exactly what it is and does. But such language is not only deficient for "Charmed magic casements, opening on the foam of perilous seas, in faery lands forlorn," it is useless to express how a man feels when he has been sullen with his wife! or to catch the little sad hint of mutability and pathos that crosses his mind when he goes back to a class reunion!

We are urged on every side to bring our speech into conformity with the common language of our world, to avoid expressions that do not "communicate," to be careful lest we suggest to the mind other than a rearrangement of its present content. Even if this were advisable (which it isn't), it is not possible. For preaching of the gospel is a declaration before it is our exhortation. It proclaims a madly holy arrangement for human lostness before it promises a power whereby the rearrangement of man's disordered house is possible. It deals with the significance of events in such a sequence as flat, episodic reportage cannot serve. Its promises are not wrung out of problems—although their lure is made sharp there—but out of Godly performances celebrated in the devotion of the church. The designative language of nature cannot contain the substance of Grace. But it can point, remember, celebrate, and hope. This is why, in the next lecture, I want to deal with certain imperatives for preaching that seem to me to arise out of the current concern of the churches for the kind of theological reflection which seeks to do justice to the kind of community the church knows herself to be.

2

THE SEARCH FOR THEOLOGICAL
METHOD, AND ITS
REQUIREMENT OF PREACHING

It is obviously possible for many ministers to keep separate their theological reading and reflection, and their preaching. Given the leaky structure of the human mind whereby contents of one area are regularly sloshing over unto others, this consistently maintained separation is an unusual feat. In trying to account for it I propose to say some things in the last lecture about practical facts in modern American church life which operate to encourage, if not to demand this deadening and guilt-begetting circumstance.

In this lecture I am proceeding on the assumption that the minister really knows that theology and preaching belong together, wants help in keeping the marriage alive and, while aware of the strain on the brain involved, is willing to endure it. The help proposed is to affirm that there is significance for preaching in the contemporary search for theological method, designate and describe an aspect of that search by reference to an impressive discussion of it, and finally delineate what its findings suggest for the public declaration of the Word.

The task of theology, as I understand it, is to make statements which clearly, intelligibly, and in just relationship set forth the content of the Christian faith as that faith is known and celebrated in the church. This definition requires that we understand theology both as a content and a task. It is a content because there is a sameness in the issues, divine and human, which it talks about, and a continuity in the substance of what it affirms about them. But it is the purpose of such statements to be intelligible; i.e., to say what is said in such a way as to communicate clearly to another mind precisely what the claim is. And because this activity goes on within a world where canons of clarity, requirements of intelligibility, and the nature of immediate human needs are in constant flux, the task of theology is a never-ending one.

In his *Seventeenth Century Background* Basil Willey asks why it was that "explanations of things which were satisfactory to one century were not satisfactory to another." To explain means to "make clear," to "render intelligible." But clarity and intelligibility is not a static quality of a statement; it is rather a quality of acceptability in a statement which quality is determined by the entire culture. "An explanation commands our assent with immediate authority when it presupposes the 'reality,' the 'truth' of what seems most real, most true. One cannot, therefore, define 'explanation' absolutely; one can only say that it is a statement which satisfies the demands of a particular time and place." [1]

The current search for a proper theological method is surely due to the fact that our generation finds older "explanations" simply not clear, intelligible, or in just proportion. There is a "disharmony between traditional explanations and current needs." Statements of one period are "felt as fact" in virtue of their congruity with the spirit, practice, and basic assumptions of a time; they are not "felt as fact" by another period because, in the

[1] Basil Willey, *The Seventeenth Century Background* (New York: Columbia University Press, 1942), p. 13.

unstoppable running of water over the dam, the spirit, practice, and basic assumption of a time became altered. The degree to which the common life is aware of this alteration has nothing to do with the case. That is why, to stay within our immediate field of preaching, justly celebrated sermons of thirty years ago, while admirable in terms of craftsmanship and witnessing vivacity, cannot be heard now as they were then. They make statements that are no longer "felt as fact"!

A proper theological method will be one that meets these conditions:

1. It must operate open-eyed in the midst of the problem of hermeneutics, or principles of interpretation, as these are propounded by the biblical record. I am assuming, of course, that the earliest record of what men affirmed the Christian faith to be is admitted as having central status.

2. It must operate with a kind of epistemology which is appropriate to the kind of events and claims which have been clearly generative, formative, and sustaining of the Christian faith and community. I choose a specific example of the contemporary search for a proper theological method not only because of its intrinsic responsibility and impressive force but because, having come to life in this school, its right to be heard will not be lightly questioned.

In 1957 Richard R. Niebuhr published his *Resurrection and Historical Reason*.[2] The argument of this book constitutes, I believe, the opening of a fresh and exciting period in American theological discussion. It does this because it is profoundly and accurately aware that the kind of thinking which declared Jesus Lord and Christ by his Resurrection from the dead is a kind of thinking which is a function of the historical consciousness of

---

[2] Richard R. Niebuhr, *Resurrection and Historical Reason* (New York: Charles Scribner's Sons, 1957), p. 49.

the community within which that claim was made. It affirms, further, what fifty years of critical biblical and historical and theological studies have made completely clear: ". . . that Christ and resurrection are inseparable, and the old dichotomy of Jesus of History—Christ of Faith does not solve this problem; it only dissolves Christ and the Church."

The theological method for which Niebuhr makes a solid and persuasive plea is so clearly set forth in certain of his own summary sentences that by putting several of them in sequence the scope and rationale of his proposal is plain. Says Niebuhr:

Certainly one of the indisputable offices of theology is to open the mind of the present community to the way in which the primitive Church apprehended the event that became the focus of its self-understanding. Any attempt to relate ourselves to the historical Jesus in a manner fundamentally alien to the experience of the New Testament church is based on a sophistical idea of history, and ultimately leads us away from the object of the quest.

In several chapters following this stated program the writer describes and analyzes nineteenth century and current ways of relating ourselves to the historical Jesus, and gives particular attention to the options elaborated in the work of Karl Barth, Rudolph Bultmann, and John Knox. He finds none of them to be adequate, and all inadequate for varieties of the same reason: they do not take seriously the kind of knowledge of Jesus the Lord which the Resurrection record assumes. Barth, because he makes an attempt ". . . to answer the methodological and historical problems raised by the nineteenth century by foreclosing all discussion of epistemological questions and insisting that the subjectivity of Jesus Christ, the God-man, is the only important reality confronting the mind of man." Bultmann's program of demythologization is assessed as inadequate because "Faith is oriented not on the picture of Jesus, but on the instantly proclaimed Word; it arises not in memory of the past, but in the

eschatological moment without past or future." And further,
". . . the real purpose of historical investigation is the discovery
of new dimensions, not in the past, but in the historian himself."
New Testament theology is thus disqualified from playing a
constructive role in the forming of a theological method which
shall take seriously the problem of faith and history, and particularly this faith, rooted as no other religious faith is, in the very
concreteness of history, and becomes nothing more than ". . . the
first permanent expression of the distinctively Christian consciousness, and begs the question of the external history of that
consciousness"[3] "thus leaving . . . theology with nothing to discussion except the human need for self-understanding in general."

The work of John Knox is given detailed attention. Its basic
thesis is that ". . . the data with which biblical theologians have
to deal . . . will become luminous only if they are approached
not as simple facts but as events." Event is, to Knox's mind, the
basic category for an analysis of history and the way in which
it is known. A historical occurrence is simply an occurrence
that was perceived and remembered. In other words, it evoked
the response of a historical subject. . . . There can be no
a-historical knowledge of a historically revealed Lord, no relationship to Jesus Christ apart from the power of memory or
from the community in which that memory is lodged.[4] This
method of interpreting the relation of faith and history, operating
with the triad—Jesus Christ • Church • New Testament—drives
the argument, by the power of its internal relations, to declare:
"The Resurrection is a part of the concrete empirical meaning
of Jesus, not the result of mere reflection upon that meaning. . . .
It was something given. It was a reality grasped in faith."[5]
When, however, one investigates where and when and what this

---

[3] *Ibid.*, pp. 57, 58.
[4] *Ibid.*, pp. 62-63.
[5] John Knox, *Christ the Lord* (New York: Harper and Brothers), p. 60.

"resurrection-event" really is, what he ends up with is the community's experience of the Christ-Spirit within it. And so adequate a transcript of the event itself is this "remembering" community that the Resurrection of Jesus is not a datum of faith but a postulate of the community's experience, and the apostolic narratives of resurrection are superfluous, from the point of men of faith.[6]

Niebuhr introduces his own constructive discussion with several statements which are not only a correct report of the biblical-theological situation in our time, but also provide material for our effort to say something useful about the theme of this lecture: what are the requirements for preaching which are suggested by this search for a proper theological method? He writes, "The impasse into which Protestant theology has come through its efforts to give significance to the resurrection tradition shows that the dogma of pure reason does not have sufficient resources to give Protestantism that kind of knowledge of Christian origins that its life and doctrine require." What is necessary, Niebuhr declares, is ". . . a critique of historical reason, a reason that will not seek the possibility of biblical history in the conditions of natural science or idealistic metaphysics, but rather in the answer to the distinctive question, how do we know historical events."[7]

How do we know historical events? That question, standing between the biblical narrative of the mighty acts of God and the existing individuals who look up at us at the moment when, having read, we close the book and begin to preach, is the question. And if the preacher does not ponder it and wrestle with it, exciting and informing his pondering and wrestling with the best resources of biblical and theological labors, then nothing really useful can be done for him. For what does it mean that

[6] *Ibid.*, p. 69.

[7] Niebuhr, *op. cit.*, p. 89.

the declared redemptive power of human life comes to us in a narrative? This: that time is the category of the historical; that because the redemptive power of God has become time, faith-engendering witness cannot be borne to that power save in a kind of preaching which is a rhetorical address to men in their time-determined and time-imprisoned existence.

There is a noetic potency in temporality. Preaching must be such an activity as invites the hearer to suspect a congruity between what is declared to have been done by God in time, and his own self-consciousness as a creature of time. By the term "creature of time" I do not refer only to the fact of duration, clock time, the observable but scarcely exciting fact that there is a before-and-after pattern in human experience. I refer, rather, to a fact that has been observed by every critic of Immanual Kant, that time and space are not comparable categories. Space is a conception. Time is a feeling. It is a word to indicate something inconceivable—a "sound-symbol"—and to use it as a notion, scientifically, is utterly to misconceive its nature. In the entire company of older philosophy I know but one profound and reverent presentation of time: it is in the fourteenth chapter of the eleventh Book of St. Augustine's *Confessions*. "Quid est ergo Tempus? Si nemo ex me quaerat scio; si quaerenti explicare velim, nescio!" (Translation—What is time then? If nobody asks me, I know; but if I were desirous to explain it to one that should ask me, I know not [Loeb Classical Library Edition]). It is possible to illustrate this statement about time in many particulars. The most quick and living way is simply to muster, for the evocative and response-begetting power they have, a miscellany from man's general confessional.

From John Milton's "Nymphs and shepherds dance no more" to our present century is a long time. And this time has seen a magnificent multiplication of devices, institutions, analgesics, and therapeutics designed to make man, the "time-creature," more content, prosperous, and secure in his "brief and mutable traject," or designed to obscure the fact of death by narcotizing the living as we cosmetize the dead. But the intervening centuries have done nothing to diminish the passion with which men regard mutability and passingness. The passion has become rather less restrained—for life can become so air-conditioned as to make its contingency seem a huge and somewhat rotten joke.

That distortion of the New Testament witness to the Resurrection of Jesus Christ (which carries its distinctiveness clearly stamped upon it) whereby its character has been translated out of particularity to the generality of immortality, makes it increasingly difficult even to declare the hope of the resurrection. For resurrection deals bluntly with man in his temporality—and claims to overcome it. Immortality deals with man in his ideal non-temporality and essays to persuade him that his actuality is not his reality. But men at whiles are sober,
And think by fits and starts.
And when they think, they fasten
Their hands upon their hearts.[8]

So it is that the facts break through, and in so doing draw out from men reflections immediate and forceful. As, for instance, the lovely "Epitaph" by Walter de la Mare:

Here lies a most beautiful lady,
Light of step and heart was she;
I think she was the most beautiful lady
That ever was in the West Country.
But beauty vanishes; beauty passes;
However rare—rare it be;
And when I crumble, who will remember
This lady of the West Country?[9]

[8] A. E. Housman, "Could Man Be Drunk?" *Complete Poems of A. E. Housman* (New York: Holt, Rinehart and Winston, Inc., 1959). Copyright 1940, 1959, by Holt, Rinehart and Winston, Inc., publishers. Reprinted by permission of the publishers.

[9] Walter de la Mare, "An Epitaph," *Collected Poems, 1901-1918* (New York: Henry Holt & Co., Inc., 1920), I, 160.

The interpretation of resurrection as merely the persistence of human or divine memories in "minds made better by their presence" can hardly persist beyond the crumbling of the rememberers.

The noetic power resident within the self's understanding of passingness must, in preaching, be conjoined to the revelationary power resident within a story of redemptive deeds accomplished in sequential, dramatic form, within time and passingness. The congruity of the two magnitudes—man's pathos and God's passion —both unfolding their power in time and history, is the most general theme of biblical preaching: it is the homiletical counterpart to the "interpretation according to historical reason" for which Niebuhr appeals. If, as he affirms, ". . . one of the indisputable offices of theology is to open the mind of the present community to the way in which the primitive church apprehended the event that became the focus of its self-understanding," so it is an indisputable office of preaching to do the same thing.[10]

But not in the same way, for theology and preaching are distinct offices of the church. It is the task of theology to keep categories clean, to explicate the faith of the church in categories which are inwardly fashioned by the particularity of the events and affirmations which are constitutive of the community of the people of God. It is the task of preaching to enflesh these categories with the living, episodic, and anecdotal concreteness of historical and present eventfulness. This concreteness does not deliver its force in a simple melody; it requires, rather, a kind of counterpoint—voices in such contrapuntal relevancy as shall fuse together the passion from above incarnately become present in order to redeem the pathos from below.

[10] It is not necessary for the sake of the present argument to share this chapter's high evaluation of Niebuhr's book, nor to consent to Niebuhr's analysis and judgment upon the ideas of others who are presently busy with biblical hermeneutics. The preoccupation of the entire theological world with this issue is a significant point.

What is required in order to move toward the accomplishment of this? As I now attempt to elaborate several requirements which that task imposes upon the preacher, it will be evident that we are still absorbed in the large figure of speech with which we began: the ecology that determines the fertility of the fields of faith. The single stone of a declaration of a specific grace, or of a promise of power, or of an all-obliterating forgiveness, or of a judgment—such single stones are set in a ring of remembered mercies. They are what they are; but what they are in their separate brightness gathers a glow and achieves a larger circle of meaning, a certain steadiness of godly fact, when set in the ring of the great story.

Two propositions indicate specifically what, in my judgment, is necessary. First, a reformation of worship whereby the noetic power of time may support the content of biblical preaching. For worship is that activity of the household of God in which the content of the moment is ensconced in the events and the remembered career of the great story.[11] Worship is personal; but it is never individual. Just as it breaks personal life open to the sweep of the arc of grace in such a way as to gather the person in all the immaculate selfhood of his particularity into the fold of the relentless Shepherd, so, with no loss of existential immediacy, it breaks open the trap of the moment to the power of the possible.

If this prospect means fresh attention to the content and role of liturgy, let us not blanch in free church horror or smilingly relax in liturgical satisfaction. We dare not blanch, for our choice is not, as one of my colleagues is wont to say, between liturgy and no liturgy; the actual choice is between liturgy

[11] I have tried to make this clear in another essay during the North American Conference on Faith and Order in Oberlin in 1957. The essay is printed as an appendix to this book. The proceedings were published as *The Nature of the Unity We Seek* (St. Louis, Missouri: The Bethany Press, 1958).

which may accomplish ecological deepening and liturgy which does not, i.e., between good liturgy and bad liturgy. If the church really is, among other things, the community that re-members Jesus, then liturgy is but the obedience of the practice of the church to the reality of its mind! And we who have grown up within the liturgical tradition dare not relax as if we, by our deeds of preservation, were automatically obedient. For a liturgical tradition, shaped for recollective vitality, may be so disengaged from the glowing stone of the instant Word as not only to fail to enshrine it but actually constitute a devout irrele-vancy. Repetition of the mellifluous can become torpor con-cealed by piety. And often does.

Recall now the evidence, illustrated previously by Niebuhr's discussion of the current theological concern with the resurrec-tion narrative in the New Testament: that teaching and preach-ing have not done with this matter. Efforts to contain the mean-ing of the church's testimony to the resurrection within various categories of interpretation have, rather, thrust its character as intransigently belonging to the realm of historical reason sharply into the center of the church's present mind. And suppose now a preacher to this moment who has followed the biblical, philo-sophical, and historical battles of the past 150 years. Suppose him, further, to be a man who is compelled so to preach the gospel of the Resurrection to the common life as not to betray in his pulpit what he learns in his study. Is it actually possible to declare the dimension of the meaning of the resurrection if that declaration is unsurrounded by, unsupported by, and, in the trans-momentary reality of worship, uninvested with the non-propositional noetic force of historical time? It is possible, yes. It is also possible to speak tenderly to a man who suddenly finds that he has but a few months to live, as if

"He were the first to ever burst Into that silent sea——"

but we commonly do not do so.

All things are more bearable if we make a story of them. And ultimate desolutions are made both bearable and significant when the story is the Ultimate Story. That is why man's time, in the Order for the Burial of the Dead, is inserted not only into its own pattern of passingness, but into God's time. That is why, whether we honor liturgical continuities or not, we enfold the broken rhythms of existence within a mightier rhythm in the words of Psalm 90:

Lord, thou hast been our dwelling place in all generations. Before the mountains were brought forth, or ever thou hadst formed the earth and the world, even from everlasting to everlasting, thou *art* God. Thou turnest man to destruction; and sayest, Return, ye children of men.[12]

How the powers of the Christian past are to be related to the living moment so as to help such a central affirmation as the Resurrection of Jesus Christ to bloom in the mind to its indeterminate dimension, I do not clearly know. But I do know that shallowly devised, mood-engendering stimulants to unstructured piety are not helpful. A structure appropriate to this substance, because recollective both of what this substantial affirmation gathers up into itself and of what affirmation and counsels flow out of it, serves to make available to the action of the Spirit the noetic powers resident in historical reason. Hundreds of years of Christian preaching have taken place in such a context; and while it is properly asserted that the erosion from the mind even of the church of the rich referents traditionally clustered about the Easter narratives makes dependence upon them questionable, it must nevertheless be pointed out that a process can be reversed.

There is heartening evidence that a biblical soil-conservation program is presently at work. The following facts support this

[12] Holy Bible, A. V.

belief: the participation of the churches in the theological conversations of the ecumenical movement, which perforce have
had to find their common starting point and common vocabulary
in biblical literature and theology; the growing body of specifically biblical theology, produced by the very vitality of frag-
mentary and monographic studies. These studies, extracting the
differentiation of the parts, and astounded nevertheless by the historical fact that there has been discernible unity transcending
them in the mind and life of the church, have thrust into the
foreground a fresh interest in the unity of the biblical tradition,
and in the doctrine of the church. To these forces from within
the churches must be added another from without. An in-
creasing body of contemporary literature has laid hold of old
biblical themes, episodes, central terms and symbols because it
finds there, presumably, stuff elemental and big enough to contain
and furnish forth its message. We remark the curious fact that
just as, thirty years ago, the churches had about succeeded in
excising Bach and Palestina from the ken of the new generation
at the moment college and high school choirs were finding them
—and church schools, afraid of the recondite reaches of the doctrine of the Lord's Supper, beheld their children at school singing "*O Magnum Mysterium*" and "*Ave, Corpus Verum*"—so, too,
the preaching fashion, having become in large part the holy
branch office of the local psychiatric clinic, is now confronted
with "*J.B.*," "*The Fall*," "*Christmas Oratoria*," and the considerable theological imagery in "*Four Quartets.*"

Easter is not an episode; it is both a culmination and a new
beginning. Resurrection is an assertion about God before it is
a puzzling reported fact about Jesus. And the persistent heart of
the puzzle is due to the fact that the first shines through the
second, and has never been understood in the historical mind of
the church in any other way. And worship in the church must
set that stone in that setting. As, for instance, in the old propers

of the missal for *Quasi Modo Geniti*, the first Sunday after Easter. By an ordered round of readings—Old Testament, Gospel, and Epistle—plus the fragments in Introit and Gradual, the church once secured the people against the poverty of the preacher; extended the orbit of this season's declaration beyond the fugitive inspiration of the moment. The Introit for that day, as indeed for the entire post-Easter season up to Ascension Day, makes clear that the One "with whom we have to do" in the resurrection is God. Here are selections from these Introits:

> The Earth is full of the goodness of the Lord:
> By the Word of the Lord were the heavens made.
> Say unto God, how terrible art thou in Thy works:
> Through the greatness of Thy power shall
> Thine enemies submit themselves unto Thee.
> O Sing unto the Lord a new song,
>   for He hath done marvelous things.
> His right hand, and His holy arm, hath
>   gotten Him the victory.
> Make a joyful noise unto God, all ye
>   lands, sing forth the honor of His name
> Make His praise glorious.

The Collect for the Day, by the very amplitude of the gift prayed for, makes clear that the deed of God's power in the Resurrection of Jesus Christ is in a continuum of grace whose endless field of operation is nothing less than the restoration of human life to its Godly intention. Profoundest theological assertions in these simple prayers are made a part of the worshipers' consciousness.

"Grant we beseech Thee, Almighty God, that we who have celebrated the solemnities of the Lord's Resurrection, may by the help of Thy grace, bring forth the fruits thereof in our life and conversations: through the same Jesus Christ . . ."

In the Introit the source of resurrection action is stated; in the Collect the scope of resurrection action is acknowledged; and

in the Epistle and Gospel lessons which follow, what is required
of the hearers is set forth. This requirement in the Gospel lesson (John 20:19-31) is stated not propositionally but in a narrative: the story of the appearance of Jesus, the disbelief of
Thomas, and the response of the Lord.

Simply to have these elements in this sequence in the single
hour of worship does not, to be sure, guarantee anything at all.
What is suggested, however, is that these words of the remem-
bering-church-in-time provide a pattern within which the nature
and size of the resurrection faith and promise is secured against
reduction and trivialization. Reformation of worship cannot con-
vey faith; it can go a considerable distance toward making clear
what the Christian object and substance of faith is.

The second proposition in which I suggest what the quest for
theological method requires of preaching is this: the pace of
historical reason, whereby ultimate meanings are disclosed, is
not the pace at which problems of faith arise; and preaching
must be a leading activity of that nurture of the church whereby
this is acknowledged and dealt with. That is to say that what
the gospel has by way of reply to a man's problem cannot be
proclaimed, disclosed in its salvatory depth, or enfold his problem in its strange reconstitutive power with the same instant
clarity and immediacy as marks the problem. What I need is
clear, immediate, and pressing: what has been accomplished and
is available for my need cannot be packaged and instantaneously
delivered as from a holy pharmacy. Problems arise in the lives
of individuals, and the terms in which the problems of faith
become articulate are a function of the total life of the generation. But the replying instruction into the faith which is the
church's true treasure is not commonly available to human need
in the clinking and separate coins of declaration, diagnosis, judgment, and grace. The need and the reply must, in the complex
ecology of faith, find their congruity. This seeking and finding

have been many times described, and G. K. Chesterton's account is a particularly moving one:

And then followed an experience impossible to describe. It was as if I had been blundering about since my birth with two huge and unmanageable machines, of different shapes and without apparent connection—the world and the Christian tradition. I had found this hole in the world: the fact that one must somehow find a way of loving the world without trusting it; somehow one must love the world without being worldly. I found this projecting feature of Christian theology, like a sort of hard spike, the dogmatic insistence that God was personal, and had made a world separate from Himself. The spike of dogma fitted exactly into the hole in the world—it had evidently been meant to go there—and then the strange thing began to happen. When once these two parts of the two machines had come together, one after another, all the other parts fitted and fell in with an eerie exactitude. I could hear bolt after bolt over all the machinery falling into its place with a kind of click of relief. Having got one part right, all the other parts were repeating that rectitude, as clock after clock strikes noon. Instinct after instinct was answered by doctrine after doctrine. Or, to vary the metaphor, I was like one who had advanced into a hostile country to take one high fortress. And when that fort had fallen the whole country surrendered and turned solid behind me. The whole land was lit up, as it were, back to the first fields of my childhood.[13]

This process, which is the inner history of every man whose life in the whole weight of its problematic character and its ambiguous self-consciousness has been lived within the sound of the voice of the Christian tradition, has a pace that is slower than the urgent haste of individual perplexities. And in every generation it is the peculiar task of preaching to lay the shape of the healing to the peculiar contours of the hurt. This ministerial task requires a double sophistication and a double pace: the

[13] G. K. Chesterton, *Orthodoxy* (New York: Dodd, Mead and Company, Inc., 1936), pp. 127 f. Reprinted by permission of Dodd, Mead & Company. Copyright 1908, 1936, by Dodd, Mead & Company, Inc.

preacher must constantly repossess with the deliberate steadiness of history's pace the accumulated resources of the fields of faith, and he must at the same time race along with his time in instant knowledge of its lusts and loves, its longing and its lostness. Only thus can he sink the moment's problems into the accumulated humus of the long history of the people of God.

3

THE ROLE OF THE IMAGINATION
IN PREACHING

PART ONE

As we now, in this chapter and the next, inquire into the role of the imagination in preaching, we may seem to have shifted from any further concern with the ideas thus far submitted and to have entered a fresh area of reflection. To do that has not been the intention; it is rather proposed in these two sections to ask and make an effort to describe and illustrate how the notion of faith as maturing in the ecology of the history of the people of God requires of preaching a vigorous and controlled use of the imagination. We have indicated under the figure of ecology in the world of nature the complex and intimate relationships operative in that process whereby Christian affirmations are made in terms integral with their status in the witnessing and remembering community, and also heard in terms which prevent their distortion into rationalistic, moralistic, naturalistic, or psychological categories. In the course of the argument the noetic force of time in the process of apprehension and the significance of the revival of liturgical worship as the church's pedagogy have been pointed out. The claim has been made that worship which thus fuses the present with the remembered past is the rich and allusive theatre within which Christian affirmations are made with an amplitude proper to their nature, and responses are invited at a level proper to their gravity.

Before we get into the argument at all it is necessary to make clear in what sense the term imagination is here used. This clarification is necessary because the term has been so debased, particularly in discourse about preaching, that it were better not to use the word at all if another were available. But no other word is available. What one must do, then, is strip from the word those connotations which make its popular use perilous for our present purpose and re-present the term in its naked intention.

Imagination is not used here to designate that mere vivacity of the mind whereby unlikely juxtaposition of things or notions imparts startling cleverness to discourse; it is not a quality produced by the accidental endowment of the temperament with whimsicality. Contemporary preaching is full of dramatic and piquant turnings of the text, irresponsible arbitrariness in strained if ever so personable interpretations of biblical figures, events, and statements. That these practices are indulged in does not define imagination; one might be so unkind as to suggest that they define the preacher.

Imagination in its proper meaning is never an addition, it is an evocation. It is perception, not piquancy. Its work is not cosmetical or decorative; it is a function of percipiency. It is exercised not only in the perception of new qualities in things, but also in the discovery of hitherto unseen relationships between things. Richard Kroner, the Gifford lecturer in 1942, concluded a long chapter on the function of the imagination in the life of faith with this paragraph:

Imagination owes its power to its peculiar nature. It is not, like sensation or intellect, confined to either the realm of sense reality or of intellectual notions and general concepts, but it belongs rather to both realms, and it is, therefore, suited to span the gulf between them. The imagination is at home in the sphere of change as well as in the sphere of changeless ideas; it is rooted as much in the visible as in the invisible world; indeed, its peculiar excellency consists exactly in its capacity of making visible what is invisible and of detecting the invisible element in the visible situation. Imagination binds together what the thinking separates; or, more precisely, it maintains the original unity of the elements separated by abstract thought. Imagination is as realistic as it is idealistic; it is as sensuous as it is intellectual; it moves in a medium in which the extremes are still united and undissolved.[1]

We move even closer to the definition of the role of imagination in preaching when we proceed from that judicious statement about general religious discourse to affirm that specifically Christian discourse is intrinsically needful of the same thing. For the central revelation of God in an Incarnation of grace in a world of nature inwardly requires that all discourse inclusive of these two magnitudes is of necessity dialectical. And imagination is the name for that category-transcending and fusing vision and speech which is proper to the given character of God's self-disclosure. The problem of proper Christian statement may be put in another way.

The "power and the truth" of the Christian gospel is in the level and the dimensions of its assault upon the hurt God-man relationship. When once it is acknowledged that man is a creature of nature who nevertheless cannot settle for the natural and that he is an object of grace who nevertheless must celebrate grace *in* the natural—it is at the same time settled that any adequate theological explication must forever be two sided; that is, dialectical. Its statements will always have to walk the knife edge at the frontier or fuse together the magnitudes of nature and grace.

This double character of Christian communication, if lost or blurred by oversimplification, banalization, or moralization, can

[1] *The Primacy of Faith* (New York: The Macmillan Company, 1943), p. 138.

perhaps achieve a hearing—but usually at the cost of the truth.
Every simple term of the faith must be set forth in such a way
that the multiple dimensions of its own content are exposed.

Faith, for an instance, is related to man's nature and his need.
But if presented as simply engendered by nature and need and
not as a faith in the faithfulness of God—that is, as trust in its
object—it is distorted into a psychological reassurance, or de-
graded into some sort of bonding agent which can then be exploited as a necessary adhesive for the wholeness of the personality.

Love is related to man's nature and need. But if presented
simply as a free-flowing human resource, itself in no need of
the fires of redemption, it becomes a name for the most adored
illusion ever to seduce mankind. Christian love is born not
simply of love itself as expanded, sensitized, or even cauterized
by suffering, but out of the love wherewith we are beloved,
wherewith we are made "acceptable in the Beloved." In the
understanding of the New Testament the passive form of the
verb is always the womb of the active.

Hope, in the Christian understanding, is not simply resolute
hopefulness. It is a "living hope" to which men have to be
"born again." Its source is not in a religiously informed and
optimistic reading of history or in the solitary human career as
this may be temperamentally disposed toward the bright side of
things. Its source is again its object, the "God of hope" who,
we pray, may "grant us joy and peace in believing."

Only this double character of the Christian faith and life can
make sense of the strange speech of the New Testament. The
world is there called our proper place of obedience, the place
where we are to "go and do likewise," the theatre in which
Christ is to be obeyed by service to "the least of these, my
brethren." And this same world as nature *and* as history is
called "no abiding city," a place of pilgrimage. It is given us as

our house precisely on the ground that it does not become our home. Every confession of Christendom stresses this double character of the Christian hope. "Not yet . . . yet even now."

These considerations add up to the judgment that while it is possible to make undialectical single statements about general idealism, for instance, it is quite another and a more imaginative task to expose the inner core of faith which looks like and works like idealism but is compounded of utterly different stuff. It is possible to expound simple moralism; it is another matter to communicate that kind of moral gravity which has no faith in morals but, being justified by faith, has a dynamics for moral responsibility that is forever confusing to the moralist! It is possible to make a moving sermon out of "bear ye one another's burdens." It is also possible to make a second equally moving sermon out of "every man must bear his own burdens." The task is considerably complicated however by faith's knowledge that both statements are fused and made concrete in a burden bearer of God's own choosing. "Then Jesus, knowing that He came from God and went to God, took a towel and girded Himself and began to wash the disciples' feet."

Because preaching presses for a God-determined and Christ-realized *ethicality*, and because the gift of grace whereby this possibility is bestowed is ensconced in a holy story, the character of Christian preaching is a unique kind of discourse. Current philosophical preoccupation with language analysis cannot, indeed, say what this discourse should be. It can, however, by its critical scrutiny designate the differences between propositions aimed at logical cognition and propositions aimed at the exposure of specifically the Christian and Christianly-ethical alternative.

Paul Holmer, in his article on "Kierkegaard and Ethical Theory,"[2] analyzes the difference in type of discourse between

---

[2] *Ethics*, an International Journal of Social, Political, and Legal Philosophy, Vol. LXIII, No. 3 (April, 1953), p. 63.

". . . those who claim cognitive significance for ethical claims and those who claim ethical and religious and metaphysical significance for logical discourse." In his exposition of Kierkegaard's writings on ethics, Mr. Holmer speaks as follows:

> Ethicality is not a matter of searching for conceptual truth; it is rather a matter of seeking to become the truth. . . . The end of the process is not, therefore, understanding as it is in the instance of all propositional truths but is rather 'becoming' something different than one was. Ethicality does not produce objective truths—it transforms the subject. The aim in ethics and religion is not to know the truth but to become it. . . . To the ethical and religious man there is no need to weep if the cognitively delineated cannot properly be called reality. . . . Needless to say this implies no derogation of science or gnosis—it means only that one does not apply intellectual criteria to all things human and that one states in a new way that man is not only a subject for knowledge but is also a subject in the process of making his own existence. Further, Kierkegaard insists that there is a kind of structuralization within the emotional cosmos, the inward life, too. Swenson has very aptly remarked that Kierkegaard has shown '. . . that the life of feeling has inherent structure and system, that valuations fall into coherent systematic groups, that emotions are not merely a structureless mush. . . .' He believes there is a kind of logos obtaining within subjectivity.

By an elaboration of two propositions I hope to illustrate the role of the imagination as it has been defined and asserted to have a proper role in preaching. The first proposition is this: that imagination invests the specifically Christian moral intelligence with perceptive sensibility.

There are places in the scripture where this "logos obtaining within subjectivity" must operate to make the mind permeable to central meaning. When Isaiah protests that "the heart of this people is fat," he is lamenting something that cannot be equated with mere intellectual lethargy, recalcitrance, or even moral perversity. He is reporting a particular instance of what is gen-

eral enough to have caused the ancient Litany of the church
to cry:

> In all time of our tribulation;
> In all time of our prosperity;
> In the hour of death;
> And in the day of judgment:
> Help us, good Lord.

There are dynamics of damnation resident in prosperity, and
they are of so sinuous and powerful a nature as to deserve acknowledgment in a series that includes tribulation, death, and
judgment. There is a fat as well as a gaunt way to go to hell.
There are stupors that obtain because of the decay, or the sheer
blubber-encasement of some natural percipiency. For this situation Isaiah could only say that hearts are fat!

The investigation of the relationship between fat and perception is not a matter, I suppose, that formal epistemology con-
cerns itself with; but in its words about the knowledge of God
the biblical account is steeped in it. And if the imagination of
the preacher does not pierce through the chinks of formal concepts and inwardly recreate what hides there, the moral heart of
the matter will remain inert. Take, for an instance, Moffatt's
vigorous rendering of Eph. 4:17-19. The writer is on the trail
of something that shows itself at the level of torpid intelligence,
loss of purpose, and the decay of common animal decency. But
he knows that these manifestations are symptomatic of some
fracture that is below and anterior to them all. He writes, therefore, to ". . . insist and protest in the Lord that you must give
up living like pagans, for their purposes are futile, their intelligence is darkened, they are estranged from the life of God by
the ignorance which their dullness of heart has produced in
them."

There is a difference between a fat heart and a dull heart. The
fat hearted are likely to be dull, but all the dull are not fat. There

can be a virtuous kind of dullness of heart; a tight-lipped, efficient, decent, and unimaginative refusal to let facts be facts or,
rather, a so contented existence within one's chosen and familiar
world of fact that equally obvious but unexpected facts are
dismissed with the same brisk impatience as a good mechanic
reveals when a bumbling apprentice hands him a wrench when
he needs the pliers. It is one among the many values I have for
a long time gained from the work of Joseph Conrad that he per-
ceives and pictures this grey kind of damnation with peculiar
clarity. Here he is in *Typhoon*, introducing the Captain:[3]

> Captain MacWhirr, of the steamer *Nan-Shan*, had a physiognomy
> that, in the order of material appearances, was the exact counterpart
> of his mind: it presented no marked characteristics of firmness or
> stupidity: it had no pronounced characteristics whatever, it was
> simply ordinary, irresponsive, unruffled.

The captain's ship was on her way to a port with some cargo
and 200 Chinese coolies returning to their village after a few
years of work in tropical colonies. When the typhoon struck,
these men, trapped in a lower deck amid a catapulting inferno
of loose sea chests and other gear, were pounded to a wounded
mass of misery. And all the time, as during the crucial hours
before, the captain simply stared at the falling barometer in sheer
refusal to open his stolid mind to the knowledge of what, even
before the storm came, he ought to have done. Conrad has, in
the body of the tale, the following paragraph. It speaks of the
China Sea and of a captain; it also speaks of the deep and un-
dramatic damnations wrought in the world by the dull and
heavy-lidded men of good will who will not look!

> The sea itself had never put itself out to startle the silent man,
> who seldom looked up and wandered innocently over the waters

[3] Joseph Conrad, "Typhoon," *Portable Conrad* (New York: Doubleday
and Company, Inc., 1959), pp. 1, 207. Reprinted by permission of J. M.
Dent & Sons, Ltd., London.

with the only visible purpose of getting food, raiment, and house-room for three people ashore. Dirty weather he had known, of course. He had been made wet, uncomfortable, tired in the usual way, felt at the time and presently forgotten. So that upon the whole he had been justified in reporting fine weather at home. But he had never been given a glimpse of immeasurable strength and of immoderate wrath, the wrath that passes exhausted but never appeased—the wrath and fury of the passionate sea. He knew it existed, as we know that crime and abominations exist; he had heard of it as a peaceable citizen in a town hears of battles, famines, and floods, and yet knows nothing of what these things mean—though, indeed, he may have been mixed up in a street row, have gone without his dinner once, or been soaked to the skin in a shower. Captain MacWhirr had sailed over the surface of the oceans as some men go skimming over the years of existence to sink gently into a placid grave, ignorant of life to the last, without ever having been made to see all it may contain of perfidy, of violence, and of terror. There are on sea and land such men thus fortunate—or thus disdained by destiny or by the sea.

There is a second way in which this proposition—that imagination invests the specifically Christian moral intelligence with perceptive sensibility—authenticates itself. We cannot come at it more bluntly and accurately than Buffon did: "The style is the man himself!" Suppose that the substance of the sermon is a section from one of the Epistles of St. Paul. The substance and the style are here so wedded that the full-blooded personal substance of what the man is saying cannot be apprehended if the imagination has not been quickened and informed by the style of the utterance. There are ways of saying this, but we shall be better instructed if we test Kroner's statement that "Imagination maintains the original unity of elements separated by abstract thought" by testing it against a concrete instance of the Pauline style.

In the whole of scripture there is perhaps no passage in which is so tightly compressed and interwoven a more various company

of massive ideas as in the eighth chapter of Romans. To make
a unity out of that complexity, a symphony out of that baffling
polyphony of powerful voices is a task before which the dissect-
ing intelligence feels its incompetence. And yet one has to know
little of Paul to know that he, who wrote this, was in no confusion. His mind, though intricate in its matter and process, was
no chaotic jumble of high epigrams. The task then is to seek
from the inside of that passage its vital motif, its invisible cohe-
sive element. And it is in this task that the imagination, if it has
been informed by acquaintanceship with the ways of men as
immemorially they have uttered in speech their turgid and passionate hearts, may silently and in strange ways come to an
apprehension of what otherwise eludes the mind.

With the character of that passage in Romans in your memory,
consider this: that there is here exhibited a quality of the mind
in its working which is not permeable to the merely analytical
intelligence. Here is a quality that inheres as much in the *how*
of a man's speech as in the *what* of it. The prose is forward
leaning, eager, exuberant—a manifestation of that end-over-end
precipitedness that Deissmann remarked in Paul's writing, and
caught in the phrase "his words come as water jets in uneven
spurts from a bottle held upside down!" By imaginative association of this peculiarity of Paul's prose with other evidences of
this quality in experience we can come close to knowing what
it was that made him write so. And when we know that, we
shall perceive in this particular instance the value claimed for
the imagination in our first proposition—perceptive clarity. For
is not this exuberance precisely what nature regularly exhibits
at every moment of arriving at something? A horse runs with
a new rhythmic vitality when he turns the last curve and
straightens out on the home stretch. This vitality is due not only
to the drive to win but arises out of something elemental—the
combination of joy and release, the sudden realization of a long

and burdening task almost done. An intricate piece of music draws its diffuse parts together in its last pages and in a muscular and positive *coda* resolves its far-wandering voices. Mighty Burke, when he "arrives" at the end of his persuasive paragraphs, gathers together his powers of thought and language for coalescence into final words of authoritative eloquence.

To have "gotten through," to have come to the end, to sense the laborious process of "working toward" about to break through into an "end achieved," is a feeling we all know. I once worked in a shop where it was my job to operate an electric drill, boring holes at marked intervals in four-by-four timbers. For the first three and half inches, it goes its way with a steady, dull growl. And then the sound becomes more open, the machine gains speed, small splinters fly as the bit bites through the last solid stuff and spins and whines with singing ease. All "arriving," all completion has this quality, whether it be a four-inch timber, a symphony, a running horse, or a work of the mind. Can you, I wonder, have failed to observe that our minds have this quality in their working? —or can we fail to catch the tempo of "arriving" in these paragraphs of the apostle? For thirty-four verses Paul's powerful mind twists and turns and torments with as mighty a complex of ideas, actions, heavenly wonders as ever lived together in a sane man's mind. His language, like thought, is muscular, contorted, and tense—but always leaning forward . . . boring . . . boring into the hard deeps of his great subject. And then, at the thirty-fifth verse, "at last he beats his music out" in that amazing march of affirmations: "What shall we say to these things? . . . . If God be for us, who shall be against us. . . ." and passes into that song of intolerable joy that ends the chapter.

Here is imagination operating exegetically to do for a passage what studious mastery of its individual parts could never accomplish. For the imagination understands that this chapter is not only argument but adoration, not a series but a sequence, not an order but an organism. Meanings "by the way" are only to be understood from the peak of spiritual song which is the brave conclusion. The ideas here are not unrelated equals pitched into a rhetorical concatenation by enthusiasm; here is, rather, the sovereignty of grace battering its way to victory through all the torments and doubts and opacities of this man's embattled soul.

In a second proposition it is possible to state how the imagination, immersed in the Pauline substance and peculiar style, works to prepare the preacher for more lively and fuller utterance of the writer's intention. The proposition is this: Imagination is the process by which there is reenacted in the reader the salvatory immediacy of the Word of God as this Word is witnessed to by the speaker.

The peculiarity of the style mirrors the fierce dialectic set up in the psyche by the invasive Word. The strange jump, the quick, unself-conscious corrections, the contradictions—these, which bring pain to the teacher of composition, bring theological light to the preacher. The natural-religious man can make a clean explication of his case; and the beatified child of grace could, presumably, write untroubled prose descriptive of his life in God. But the Epistles of Paul stand at the intersection of nature and grace. They are the utterances of a man drawn taut between the huge repose of "a man in Christ" and the huge realism of a man of flesh and earth. It's the same man at the same time bearing witness to an inseparable movement of faith who can say: "Wretched man that I am. . . . There is therefore now no condemnation." "I don't care what you think of me. . . . I am troubled about what you think of me". Work out your own salvation in fear and trembling because no man can work out his own salvation and does not have to, for God is at work in you!

Preaching dare not put into unbroken propositions what the tormented peace of simultaneous existence in nature and grace can utter only in broken sentences. What God has riven asunder let no preacher too suavely join together. When we find, as we regularly do, that Paul stops the forward rush of active-voice statements to crack the integral structure of the affirmation with a joyous and devout regrounding of everything he is saying in the ultimacy of the passive voice, then we are obliged to stop with him. The salvatory power of the Word of God is eloquent precisely at the embarrassed halt. Where grammar cracks, grace erupts.

"I know," says Paul. And then he reflects upon what he knows, how he came to know it, and what kind of a religious confidence it was within which such knowledge occurred. The reflection stops the assertion cold, and he writes, "I mean, rather, that I have been known."

"I love," says Paul. And then he reflects upon how he came to the point where he can say that, by virtue of what startling and reconstitutive convulsion it has been made possible, and he stops the active voice in the remembrance of ". . . this Son of God who loved me, and gave himself. . . ."

"I accept," says Paul. And then the reflection! And in the course of it the remembrance of the forgiving madness of the Holy which is the creator of all sanity, the huge and obliterating acceptance by God which empowers all acceptances among men. The passive both destroys and recreates the active in its own image; and the Christian life is spun on the axis of this holy freedom whose one end is sunk in the accepting mercy of God, its other end in the need of man for an ultimate acceptance.

This transformation of the realm of the active by the power of the passive is a key not only to isolated fragments of Paul's witness, but also to an understanding of the man's total bearing within the world of nature and history. A peculiarly illuminating instance of this transformation is the memorable passage near the end of the Philippian letter. "Finally, brethren, whatever is true, whatever is honorable, whatever is just, whatever is pure, whatever is lovely, whatever is gracious, if there is any excellence, if there is anything worthy of praise, think about these things."

This paragraph, occurring as the summary of the argument of the entire Epistle, is strange. It's almost as if Paul had forgotten what he had written, or taken back what he had so passionately affirmed, or suddenly replaced his intense and consecrated gaze by a genial and relaxed smile. For three chapters he has hacked away at the adequacy of all the confidences and solidities of religion, morality, culture. I count everything as loss . . . even as refuse, he says—and drills through to the "surpassing worth of knowing Christ Jesus my Lord. . . . that I may know him and the power of his resurrection, and may share his sufferings, becoming like him in his death, that if possible I may attain the resurrection from the dead."

And then the shift. From the packed and intense inwardness of that statement, which locates the dynamics of the faith-full life of the Christian within the enacted morphology of the Incarnation and resurrection he passes, after sundry personal and admonitory asides, to the blithe and humane: "Finally, brethren, whatever is true, whatever is honorable, whatever is just, whatever is pure, whatever is lovely. . . ."

This change in tone is not a shift in center. It is, in fact, not a shift at all. It is simply the language of a man who raises his eyes from the center to the circumference. It is the maturation of centered faith into a kind of evangelical humanism. It is rhetorical celebration of a basic Christian paradox: The way to breadth is by the road of narrow concentration; the road to beauty, graciousness, justice is a road that begins with the beauty of holiness, the graciousness of Grace, the justice of judgment. The really humane is a function of the fully human; the fully human is beheld and bestowed in the new man who is the second Adam who, obedient in Gethsemane, restores to God and to himself the first Adam, faithless in Eden.

These too brief samplings of the Pauline style, while sufficient perhaps to make our formal point, suggest further and more subtle things to be learned from the Apostle to the Gentiles. To these we shall give some attention in the next. But these do suffice to bring under question the venerable practice of preaching from isolated texts, or even brief pericopes. This practice, perilous enough when exercised upon the Gospels, is intrinsically disastrous when applied to the Epistles of Paul. For to a degree unmatched in the world's literature, anything the man wrote has to be made luminous in the glow of everything he wrote. The apparent unsystematic of his language must be inwardly controlled and ordered by the central systematic of his passion. And he is the first to protest that this passion is a passive; that it is God's before it is his, and that it is his only because God's passion became a historical fact in a locatable garden.

4

THE ROLE OF THE IMAGINATION
IN PREACHING

In our effort thus far to describe and illustrate the role of the imagination in preaching, we have considered two aspects of its power: the investiture of the Christian moral vision with such sensibility as sometimes enables it to enclose within the meaning of the Word of God the subtler perditions that stalk men's lives; and the power to behold, and in part reenact, the architectonic structure of grace that is the subliterary matrix out of which the witness emerges.

In this lecture I propose to set out on the trail of two other, and trans-intellectual, powers of the imagination; and I confess that I am by no means certain of my ability to catch them in language. But the role they play in the preparation of the mind for preaching is so large and pervasive that it were better to fail to do adequate justice to them than to ignore their existence. It ought not be necessary to say that the process I am about to describe does not commonly take place in the absence of fundamental disciplines in theological work. In such disciplines freight is delivered at the unpublic back door of the mind, and is undramatically stored in the basement; it nonetheless determines what gets on the shelf and over the counter. Exegesis, and biblical-introductory studies do not guarantee a rich life to the imagination. But they do supply the mind with solid and responsible stuff, tighten thought to the particularity of the biblical speech, discourage that too-quick translation of quite specific terms into feckless generalities which makes much preaching both dull and inaccurate—and dull because inaccurate.

Let us, therefore, boldly plunge into the first of these with an experimental proposition. If the outcome does not secure the fox it may at the least indicate the direction of his flight when last seen. The imagination has the power to extend intelligibility beyond the launching site—where one can see and hear clearly, experimentally confirm confidently — into nonverifiable orbits which are nevertheless continuous with the instantly intelligible.

Concrete analysis alone can be useful here. I ask you therefore to consider the first twenty-seven verses of chapter 1 of St. Paul's Philippian letter. It was as a parish pastor preaching my way straight through this Epistle in a series of sixteen sermons that I first became aware of this orbit-tracking power of the imagination.

These verses are a rhetorical unit. The apostle, about to send back with Epaphroditus a letter to his particularly beloved Philippians, begins with a wonderfully warm and candid confession of how he feels and prays and hopes about them. He goes on to report that a jail which was intended to stop his witness has provided it rather with strange new occasions. The local situation is filled out in some detail; and in the course of this report, the more moving because unintended, the apostle discloses the mature stance of a man "in Christ" as he lives out his obedience in the midst of envy, rivalry, misunderstanding, and considerable interparty slugging.

Thus far the described situation can count upon confirmatory experience in the life of every man. Not many men, to be sure,

win through to the surging victory of Paul of Tarsus as we
hear him speak of his life within and simultaneously above a
double imprisonment. He was literally imprisoned; and he dis-
misses the fact with the light phrase, "what has happened to me."
And he was imprisoned with no opportunity to talk back to
those who, taking advantage of the stilling of a vigorous voice,
"proclaim Christ out of partisanship." Knowing what we do
about Paul—his impatience, his quick and searing temper, his
earthy inclination to slap down the opposition—we are the more
edifyingly astonished by the utter levity of the phrase in which
he sums up the whole miserable business and tosses it away.
"*Ti gar*," he says; and the only idiomatic translation that does
justice to that magnificent gesture is "So what!"

Now with all of that every man has experiences which, however limited, make Paul's victory intelligible. Every man has
that which responds to, because it is continuous with,

> The slings and arrows of outrageous fortune, . . .
> The heart-ache and the thousand natural shocks
> That flesh is heir to, . . . the proud man's contumely,
> The pangs of dispriz'd love, the law's delay,
> The insolence of office, and the spurns
> That patient merit of the unworthy takes, . . .
>
> SHAKESPEARE[1]

We probably, however, have not been able to manage the apostolic freedom of the "*Ti gar*," much less the positive, tight-lipped
breakthrough to the superlative fact that curls up all lesser
facts—" . . . whether in pretense or in truth, Christ is proclaimed:
and in that I rejoice." Not able, perhaps, to follow; but able
to understand.

But follow now the curve of the thought as Paul without a
trace of cant or self-consciousness takes off from the confirming
field of our common experience and beats out the music of his

[1] From Hamlet's soliloquy, *Hamlet* (1603), Act III, scene ii, lines 66 ff.

ultimate joy. The authentic continuity and power of this utterance is enhanced because it is flung in the face of certain persecution, probable death. "Yes, and I shall rejoice. For I know that through your prayers and the help of the Spirit of Jesus Christ this will turn out for my deliverance, as it is my eager expectation and hope that I shall not be at all ashamed, but that with full courage now as always Christ will be honored in my body, whether by life or by death. For to me to live is Christ, and to die is gain. If it is to be life in the flesh, that means fruitful labor for me. Yet which I shall choose I cannot tell. I am hard pressed between the two. My desire is to depart and be with Christ, for that is far better. But to remain in the flesh is more necessary on your account." [2]

It would be untrue to call that passage intelligible to us in the sense that the preceding verses are intelligible. By participation in Paul's Christ I too know something about liberation from the tyranny of environment, and some measure of liberation from the terrible interior tyranny of my own egocentricity. With both of these I have a measure of continuity in experience. When Paul says that because of Jesus Christ he will rejoice, I too, however faintly, can second the motion—and out of comparable experience. The trajectory of the man's thought sends his song of rejoicing into the black heavens of death, and sends back from his reflections upon it a gallant but only partly intelligible music.

This apostolic affirmation often has been wrongly compared with Socrates' words in the *Apology*, or these of John Keats:

> . . . for many a time
> I have been half in love with easeful Death,
> Called him soft names in many a mused rhyme,
> To take into the air my quiet breath;
> Now more than ever seems it rich to die,
> To cease upon the midnight with no pain, ...[3]

[2] Phil. 1:19-24.
[3] "Ode to a Nightingale" (written in 1819), vs. 6.

It won't do; and no analogy that does not center upon the concretion of love in Jesus Christ will do. Socrates died with poised nobility because that way of dying was alone congruent with his way of thinking; his surmise about life after death was a rational one, and he died supported by its power. In awful sobriety and total involvement with the ultimate issue he had made his choice. Keats' gesture is gallant, too; but on different grounds. "O for a life of sensations rather than thoughts," he once wrote to a friend. And now, with the days running out and a fated love hopeless, he longs but to dismiss all possibilities together, to "cease upon the midnight with no pain."

Tautly drawn between life and death, both men decide; on different grounds, to be sure, but on grounds comprehensible from within the generality of human experience. But what meets us in Paul's monologue about life and death is precisely the absence of any concern with these alternatives as ultimate at all! It is as if the twin tyranny of life and death had been already overcome, as if the monologue were being carried at a high remove. With an air that one can only call evangelical insouciance the man talks about living or dying as a mere tactical consideration of no central importance. The very language has the character of the muttering of a man at a hat counter hurrying to decide for the brown one or the gray one so that he might be off to some matter of genuine importance.

The point of this is that the entire orbit of the utterance is the creation of the gospel; what can be experientially confirmed does not reach the dimension of the ecology of the faith. The speaker is continuous with himself. The Paul whose participation in Christ enables him to talk about death in a way that is unintelligible to the preacher is the same Paul who talks about the praetorian guard in a way that is intelligible. And any understanding of preaching which would ignore the extension of the intelligible line and restrict Catholic witness to the dimensions of accidental experience is a thin and reductive misunderstanding.

For the gospel, when we attend to its rich and various working out in the testimony of the church has a morphology which is vaster than any man's life and a momentum which unfolds beyond any man's experience. What we know points the direction for, and in its fragments authenticates, what as yet we do not know. The gospel is not a holy box of divine propositions ranging from simple to complex; it is nothing less than the organic life of God confronting us now here, now there. But wherever we confront it we find it to be like an outcropping of a continuous vein of silver, and years and discipline and prayer and grace disclose its subterranean continuities. Or, to change the figure, it is like a tight unfolding chrysalis whose most huge promise is continuous with its most plain gift. "This, then," said Luther, "is the nature of faith: that it dares on the basis of God's grace, and creates tranquility and trust toward Him; and thinks without doubt that God will regard and not forsake it. For true faith doubts not God's good and gracious will. Such a confronted trust, or repose in God—that is Christian faith and good conscience in the scriptures. Faith does not demand anything but freely surrendered and joyously daring trust upon his unfelt, untried, and unknown goodness." [4]

We conclude then our consideration of the first proposition: that the imagination has the power and, I would now add, the witnessing duty to extend intelligibility beyond the launching site where one can see and hear clearly, or experimentally confirm into non-verifiable orbits which are nevertheless continuous with the instantly intelligible. And add to our basic figure of the ecology of the faith a second drawn from mathematics. *Extrapolation* is defined as "the calculation, from the values of a function known within a certain interval of values of its argu-

[4] *WA* 10:2, p. 239.

ment, of its value for some argument value lying without that
interval."

This extrapolation of a fragment of the knowledge of God
into its full orbit is precisely the process by which the primitive
Christians affirmed that God was in Christ. Distilled out of the
centuries of Israel's experience of the relentless and steadfast
mercy of her God is the powerful and pathetic figure in second
Isaiah. The shape of that fragment is extended to a full orbit
when the community, made a community by the words, the
work, the living presence of Jesus, bore witness to the size of
the event itself. "God hath visited his people," say the Synoptics.
"The Word became flesh and dwelt among us," says John. "For
in him the fullness of God was pleased to dwell," says Paul. It is
required of the preacher that he so master as positively to reenact this creative process whereby the witness was originally
uttered that in his witness to it the epic be not lost in the episodes,
the fullness forgotten in the fragments.

All that has been said thus far has been controlled by the figure
with which we began—the ecology of faith. So to understand
the faith of the church leads one to understand the preaching
task as a function of that context. Added to that in my own life
is a strong historical consciousness, the dominant role of biblical
theology, the catholic character of a liturgically nurtured piety
always providing promptings that are secret because they are of
the church's wholeness. Inevitable, too, that one so placed and
formed within the life of the church should practice preaching
as an effort to rebuild the topsoil of memory on the eroded fields
of faith in the hope that unfurnished poverty might be supplied.

But there are facts before us, and neither the richness of a
tradition nor the vigor of a hopeful effort can evade them. Just
as theological reflection is today dominated by the fact that the
entire mental, emotional and image context of the past is eroded,
so a way of preaching proper to that fact must be wrought out.

Our preaching, as a matter of fact, is deepeningly directed; not as the New Testament writer has it, "from faith to faith," but from faith to unfaith. Most of my preaching in the last fifteen years has been in academic chapels. And while I know that the student group represents in a more aware way the erosion to which we have alluded, the process is general.

"The world," as Dietrich Bonhoeffer has said, "has come of age." Traditional cultural and intellectual companions of the Christian gospel have been either violently destroyed or gone silently out of mind. The venerable discipline of philosophical inquiry no longer makes affirmations beyond the methodological, has curved inward upon itself. The sheer vitalities of culture, once hailed as redemptive, have for a hundred years been unpacking the logos of contradiction that infects all historical life. The very ethos of religious sentiment has on the one hand become so disenchanted as to assess its former friendliness to Christianity as false, febrile, or indecent, or, on the other, undergone a transformation whereby its terms have been instrumentally debased into techniques for integrating the personality, or into glue to hold the republic together.

> We were always able to say: 'We are children of God,
> And our Father has never forsaken His people.'
> But then we were children: That was a moment ago,
> Before an outrageous novelty had been introduced
> Into our lives . . . .
> Just how, just when It succeeded we shall never know:
> We can only say that now It is there and that nothing
> We learnt before It was there is of the slightest use,
> For nothing like It has happened before.
>
> W. H. Auden[5]

Nothing constructive is accomplished by lamenting the dissolution of structures and sentiments that once were suasions within

[5] "For the Time Being," *Collected Poems* (New York: Random House, 1945), p. 410.

which the Christian story was relevant. There is, indeed, much that is diagnostic and clarifying in the exposure of their merely suasive and mutable character. The history of Christianity is the story of the waxing and the waning of these tactical and interim alliances. As these have arisen, flourished, affirmed adequacy, they have underlined congruities between the shape of the Kerygma and the shape of the mind and spirit of the age. But these alliances come and go; and knowledge of that fact does not depress the theologian in his work but rather clarifies what that work is, urges it to its doing, and defines its limit.

Protestant theology at this moment is employed in reconstructing its method in open disengagement from all previous alliances. This radical undertaking has been forced upon it by such a multiplicity of facts and forces as would go beyond the scope of these lectures and my competence to describe. But something of their character and force can be suggested by two generalizations: 1) the full range of biblical studies has so profoundly unfolded the matrix out of which the biblical witness was fashioned that the problem of hermeneutics is of absolute urgency; and 2) the very body of reactions and the vocabulary with which our time is aware of itself is so radically strange to the world view of the Bible and to the vocabulary of all previous theological discourse as to force us, both as preachers and as teachers, to fresh foundational work.

For engagement, then, with the powers of irrelevance, incomprehension, denial, and of sheer emptiness, a new work of the imagination is required both of the theologian and the preacher. When an age matures to a point where it displays a radical transference of interest, and when its very language reveals that what former times felt as fact are no longer so felt, then the central task is clearly exposed. Demythologization as a biblical program inevitably begets symbolization as a theological program. When, that is to say, it becomes the effort of biblical theology to penetrate to the divine realities, forms, and intentions that have been temporally invested in reportorial forms available to the moment, it becomes the principal effort of systematic theology to interpret the biblical story in amplest symbolic dimensions. When myth is the term for the story, symbol is its vocabulary.

The possibilities of this way must be responsibly exploited; to do so is the given theological task of our time. And protests against the effort can be constructive only if they participate in the effort, gather up into their own vision the deepening disclosure of the symbolic and transhistorical vitalities of historical fact. Only by a thoroughgoing exploitation of the relation of reported fact and reflectively engendered meaning can the church learn how to bear witness to the mystery of her life. And she need not fear, either, that radical phases of this program which seem to dissolve the very matrix of things given in time and place will prevail for the destruction of her message. For historical fact, while quiet and infinitely patient of flexion, is tough. Historical actuality is deceptively acquiescent, but it will not, like a family dog, roll over and play dead. For there is a built-in dialectic that controls the process of historical interpretation: Fact must be expanded to symbol in order fully to announce fact; and symbol must be rooted in fact in order to retain force as a symbol.

These considerations lead us to the second proposition of this lecture. Ultimate negations generate a strange addressability by ultimate affirmations. It is not proposed here to explain that proposition; its primal spring is nowhere this side of *Credo in Deum Patrem Omnipotentem, Factorem coeli et Terrae!* It is only proposed to state it, report upon evidences that it is so, and suggest how it specifies for the contemporary preacher his stance and his tactic.

Let us consider these terms in order. Stance is posture assumed in readiness for indeterminate but resolute action. It designates how a man stands in the midst of his time, both a product of his time and, because he has a burden and a duty, alert to address his time. Stance is both poised and utterly incalculable; poised because of a knowledge of what must be done, incalculable because the how of the doing is an emergent of a fluctuant situation. Michelangelo's Moses has posture and presence, his David has stance.

The posture of the preacher is given in the substance of the faith; where he stands and what he has to say standing there are products of the attested gifts and the million-voiced responses of the centuries of the faith. But the stance of the preacher is determined by the depth with which he is penetrated by and participates in the vitalities of his time. Men of our time will not entertain as a possibility the redemption we proclaim if our stance does not reveal our involvement in the damnations they suffer. Nor will evangelical replies be accredited as possibilities if our presentation of them be not informed by involvement in the questions to which they are addressed. "God Himself Is Present" is no longer a sensible song for a congregation that is regularly addressed as if its members had never felt that God himself is absent! One need not, indeed cannot, go to school to all the lashing literature of our time in which the absence of God is celebrated. But by this means or another one must learn the lessons the schools talk about. One need not necessarily join Salinger's Holden Caulfield in the Roxy gallery, watch the Rockettes make their peculiar obeisance to the Incarnation in a tinselled Christmas routine, and hear the lad remark, lonely and honest amidst the gurgling delight of the audience, "Good ol' Jesus would a' puked!"—one need not know that particular incident. But one must by some means come to the place where he penetrates with his mind and learns his preaching stance by pondering the meaning of that bitter statement. For that trenchant remark discloses both the appalling insensibility of our time and a strangely persistent longing for righteousness.

Our proposition—that ultimate negations generate a strange addressability by ultimate affirmations—requires then a stance learned in existence always open and alive. But a stance is not a sermon. The actual sermon will be the effort we make—the tactics we employ to set over against the negations, whether they be conscious and articulate or unconscious and weary—the powers, claims, promises, and gifts of the Christian gospel. If the world has indeed come of age, and in that maturity left behind effective beliefs, remembrances, hopes that were once the humane context in which life heard the message of God's redemption, how can one preach at all? What possible tactic is there for relating possibilities to negations?

A clue is given in an observation. If one reflects upon the literature of the last three decades or so in which Christian terms have been employed to suggest the redemptive truth of the Chrisian faith, he makes an important discovery. Neither the presumed religion of Jesus, nor isolated episodes of his career, nor specific items in his teaching are the substance being pondered by the writer. What is being pondered, and that with a power and a fascination altogether singular, is the congruity between the entire story as objectively related and celebrated in the Christian church, and the whole story of man's passional subjectivity. The mighty descending, crucified, and ascending curve of love's restorative action as it invades, reenacts, and lifts back up to itself the entire human situation—this is the central theme of an impressive body of contemporary reflection. I name here a few instances, the list could be very long: *He Came Down From Heaven* and *Descent Into Hell,* by Charles Williams. *Christmas Oratoria,* with its poetic refashioning of the Kierkegaardian dialectic, and *For the Time Being,* by W. H. Auden. T. S. Eliot concludes his *Four Quartets* with lines which are both a summary of his analysis and an announcement of a salvation:

> Who then devised the torment? Love.
> Love is the unfamiliar Name
> Behind the hands that wove
> The intolerable shirt of flame
> Which human power cannot remove.
> We only live, only suspire
> Consumed by either fire or fire.[6]

These lines are a tight counterpoint in which a big theme is condensed: life's affirmative fire is only to be redeemed from self-incineration when it is met by, controlled, and purified by the God who is a consuming fire, in his concreteness of love in Christ ("I come to bring fire upon the earth") and mediated by the Spirit,

> . . . also a fire, *Veni Creator Spiritus.*
> Come, Holy Ghost, our souls inspire,
> And lighten with celestial fire;

And so, writes a contemporary poet,

> . . . while the light fails
> On a winter's afternoon, in a secluded chapel
> History is now and England.
> With the drawing of this Love and the voice of this calling.[7]

There is a preacher in the Christian church, dead now for a hundred years, who better than any other can be our tutor as we seek to learn how to preach to our time. He saw with absolute clarity that preaching is neither the bestowal of faith nor the heavenly confirmation of human truth. He understood it as a kind of "indirect communication" whereby the sluggish self is made passionately aware that its highest perfection is its need for God. Sören Kierkegaard understood that preaching cannot deliver what the need discloses; it is the function of preaching

[6] *The Complete Poems and Plays, 1909-1950* (New York: Harcourt, Brace & Co., 1952), p. 144.

[7] *Ibid.*

rather so to tell the story that God's deed becomes a possibility for man's need. He understood that preaching is a kind of contrapuntal exercise directed not primarily to a cognitive relation to the declaration, but directed rather to such evocation of the passion of the self that it shall "will" to become the truth which Christ was and is.

There is a contemporary poem which illustrates our proposition: that ultimate negations generate a strange addressability by ultimate affirmations. Its title is "Elegy: Separation of Man from God." In the poem the fact of separation is not only acknowledged, but the terms in which it is objectified are named with stunning precision. The absence of God generates a negative capability to recognize the formal adequacy of God. In the first stanza the bitter identification of opposites suggests the shape and the depth of a need to which nothing less than eucharist will be redemptive:

> These errors loved no less than the saint loves arrows
> Repeat, Love has left the world. He is not here.
> O God, like Love revealing yourself in absence
> So that, though farther than stars, like Love that sorrows
> In separation, the desire in the heart of hearts
> To come home to you makes you most manifest.
> The booming zero spins as his halo where
> Ashes of pride on all the tongues of sense
> Crown us with negatives. O deal us in our deserts
> The crumb of falling vanity. It is eucharist.[8]
>
> GEORGE BARKER

In the last stanza the poet invents a series of epithets in which are flung out, in more brutal terms than the ordinary man would permit himself, what nevertheless the ordinary man knows to be his argument with God. The startling reversal in the last line,

[8] Oscar Williams (ed.), *The Golden Treasury* (New York: Mentor Books, 1943), No. 90. Reprinted by permission of Criterion Books, Inc., New York.

in which the word God, spelled backward, is *dog,* utters the promise that time and grace can disgorge the massive need of men's souls out of their knotted negations, and find again a fierce salvation in the ancient story. Hear the epithets spat out in passion, and hear these current negations declare their kinship with all who, walking in darkness, have seen a great light. Darkness does not make a light out of sheer darkness, but darkness has a way of making light a term of passion.

> Incubus. Anaesthetist with glory in a bag,
> Foreman with a sweatbox and a whip. Asphyxiator
> Of the ecstatic. Sergeant with a grudge
> Against the lost lovers in the park of creation,
> Fiend behind the fiend behind the fiend behind the
> Friend. Mastodon with mastery, monster with an ache
> At the tooth of the ego, the dead drunk judge:
> Wheresoever Thou art our agony will find Thee
> Enthroned on the darkest altar of our heartbreak
> Perfect. Beast, brute, bastard. O dog my God!

Sometimes a spontaneous and uncalculated word may be more revelatory than one born of conscious reflection. Not long ago, in a class in systematic theology, I was speaking of the doctrine of the Holy Trinity. The effort was to disabuse the mind of some students that the doctrine had been imposed as a kind of perverse sophistication upon the assumed "simplicity" of the religion of Jesus. After an indication of the multiple strands in the New Testament witness that made this assumption questionable, and some treatment of the primitive Christian experience of Jesus Christ which invited the mind to other than monodimensional terms for a just understanding of this encounter, we moved on to a consideration of the role of the doctrine in Christianity's penetration of classical culture. I referred the students to Charles N. Cochrane's lucid description of this process[9] and for about

[9] In his *Christianity and Classical Culture* (New York: Oxford University Press, 1944).

half an hour did an enthusiastic recapitulation of Cochrane's argument: that the doctrine of the Trinity was alone a principle big enough to fill the intellectual, moral, and emotional space left by the waning ideal of *Romanitas;* and that it had, in fact, accomplished this for many men and for hundreds of years.

There sat before me a student who, in his own experience of an eroded Christian ethos and understanding and in his equally certain longing to find a faith with a magnitude equal to his problems, was a living symbol of millions in our generation to whom the gospel must be preached. When the lecture was finished—and without meaning, I think, to be overheard—he uttered a sentence monumental in its meaning for the preacher: "If it were true, 'twould do!"

There you have it—both the nature of the contemporary preaching situation and the implied tactic. We can cause no man to permit his life to be determined by the revelation of Jesus Christ as the coming of God to him. We cannot, that is to say, guarantee the victory of the truth by the telling of the story. To accomplish that is the work of the Holy Spirit. But we can so tell the story within the house of negation and empti-ness that the great passion lay its hand upon the wan, quiescent, or aggressive passions that the hearer might exclaim, "If it were true, 'twould do!"

5

MACERATION OF THE MINISTER

This lecture is not continuous with the preceding ones. It is related to them, however, because I have been aware in the preparation—with a clarity amounting to a sense of guilt—that urgings toward the kind of study and reflection presupposed for preaching to our situation have a bright and bitter sound to many who have done me the courtesy to listen. Bright because what I have called attention to is acknowledged as necessary for obedient preaching; bitter because the church, which might be expected to encourage and protect the minister in his cultivation of these conditions, does nothing of the sort.

What I have to say in this lecture might well come under an epigram applied to the Korean War: the wrong war against the wrong enemy at the wrong place! The situation I propose to describe is already and painfully well known to the clergy, and if a lecture to them has only an intermural value they are perhaps comforted in their pain by the knowledge that others know of it. It is nevertheless said here on the purely tactical ground that someone ought to speak up against what I call the maceration of the minister. He ought to do so with plain, reportorial force, and he ought to do it not as a psychologist, internist, or time-study expert—but as a churchman within the context of a convocation traditionally concerned with the practical wellbeing of the churches.

I have sought for a less violent term to designate what I behold, and maceration was the only one sufficiently accurate. Among the meanings of the term listed in the dictionary is this grim one: *to chop up into small pieces.* That this is happening to thousands of ministers does not have to be argued or established; it needs only to be violently stated. His time, his focused sense of vocation, his vision of his central task, his mental life, and his contemplative acreage—they are all under the chopper. Observation leads me to conclude, too, that this fact is general. The man who looks back thirty years to his ordination is in no better circumstance than the man who looks back three years. The man who is minister in an established parish and surrounded with a staff has substantially the same complaint as the mission minister with his self-propelled mimeograph. Nor does the church body in which the man is a minister, or the distinction or obscurity of the school which awarded him his Bachelor's degree in Divinity make any perceivable difference.

The Niebuhr-Williams-Gustafson study[1] of several years ago makes it unnecessary to dilate upon this first point. Because these men are members of theological faculties their observations were related with particular force to the responsibilities of theological educators. They therefore made quietly and with becoming academic restraint a point that I want to make noisily.

What the schools elevate the actual practice of the ministry flattens. The schools urge to competence in the various fields of theological study. The canons of competence that determine the churches' practice are not only strange to what the schools supply and encourage, they are radically destructive of their precedence and nurture. There is something positively sardonic

[1] H. Richard Niebuhr, *The Purpose of the Church and Its Ministry* (New York: Harper and Brothers, 1956).

in a quick jump from a remembered student in a remembered classroom to the same man in his parish. I have done many such jumps and the effect is disheartening. In the classroom he was told that the *basilia tou Theu,* for instance, is a phrase of enormous scope and depth, and that his declaration of it should be informed by such studies as we could expose him to in class. It was further urged that such study ought persist throughout life. His teachers were concerned that he not become so insensible as to make such easy identifications with the kingdom of God as characterize the promotional theological literature of our burgeoning churches.

Visit the man some years later in what the man still calls inexactly his study and one is more than likely to find him accompanied by the same volumes he took with him from his student room. And filed on top of even these are mementos of what he is presently concerned with: a roll of blueprints, a file of negotiations between the parish, the bank, and the Board of Missions, samples of asphalt tile, and a plumber's estimate.

When one wonders what holds the man together, enables him to bring equal enthusiasm to his practical decisions and his pastoral and proclamatory function, one learns that he is held together (if he is) by his public role of responsibility for the external advancement of the congregation. The terms in which this advancement are commonly assessed seep backward and downward to transform his interior relation to his studies. Those studies become less and less an occupation engaged in or intrinsic to his role as witness to the gospel and pastor to people, and become more and more frantic efforts to find biblical, or theological, generalities which will religiously dignify his promotional purposes. The will of God has got to be simplified into a push for the parish house. The Holy Spirit is reduced to a holy resource which can be used as a punch line for the enforcement of parish purposes. The theme of Christian obedience must be stripped of its judging ambiguities and forthwith used as a lever to secure commitment which is somehow necessarily correlated with observable services to the current and clamant program. The message, in short, is managed in terms of its instrumental usefulness for immediate goals. "Arise, and let us go hence" becomes a text so epigramatically apt that it were a shame to lose it by the complication of context or exegesis.

Where are the originating places of this process, and what forms does it take? There are, I think, three that are so obvious and constant that they can be named and described. But even these are to be recognized as functions of a force that is pervasive, and underlies them all. This basic force is a loss of the sense of the particularity of the church, the consequent transformation of the role of the minister into that of a "religious leader," and the still consequent shift whereby the ministry is regarded as a "profession" and theological education has come to understand its task as "professional education". Had this shift in meanings not occurred the three specific forces I am about to name could hardly have been effective. But the shift *has* occurred—and the minister *is* macerated by pressures emanating from the parish, the general church bodies, and the "self-image of the minister."

The Parish: The very vocabulary that has become common is eloquent. The parish has a "plant," its nature or purpose is specified in terms of a "program" for which a "staff" is responsible to a "board." The "program" is evaluated in terms of palpable production which can be totaled with the same hard-boiled facticity as characterizes a merchandising operation—and commonly is. The minister, like it or not, is the executive officer. I know of a synod of a church body which, wishing to put the matter of financial support of the "program" of the church on a less obviously allocated basis than characterizes the property tax office of the municipality, came up with a "fresh" idea: each should give as the Lord had prospered him—the synod called it the "Grace system"!

This systematization of the holy betrays, if nothing worse, a peculiar atrophy of a Protestant sense of humor. Our theology of stewardship is pragmatically translated into terms and operational devices which deny the theology we affirm. The path to such practices is easily discernible. After a generation or two in which paid quartets, in the better-heeled parishes, praised God weekly as surrogates for the congregation, and professional organizations raised the money for "plant expansion" (all, of course, with a well-oiled unction that would have glazed the eyeballs of St. Paul) it is not surprising that the counsel to stewardship should be preceded, according to some church programs, by an inquisatorial scrutiny of the share of each of the sheep in the gross national product. The reply, of course, is that it works. There can be no doubt that it does. The same reply, however, if made normative for the truth of the entire nature and scope of the meaning of the church would indicate that the theology of prayer ought to take account of the reported correlation between petition and the growth-rate of potted plants.

The Christian community always walks close to the edge of superstition, magic, and the strange human desire to translate grace into nature by a direct and forthright program. There is a relation between an immeasurable gift of grace and the responding gifts of man to advance the institutional celebration of the gospel of Grace. But it is the task of theology, as it ought to be a concern of planned parish preaching and instruction, to witness to this grace in such a way as to raise Christian eyebrows over every perverting proposal to mechanize it.

There is no evidence that policy preserves against perversion. A church in a surplice is as easily seduced as a church in a black robe, or one with neither of these. That the "business of America is business" has bequeathed to us all a vocabulary, a point of view, canons of evaluation that are so deeply rooted in our parishes that perhaps nothing short of a Kierkegaardian attack upon Christendom will suffice for renovation.

The General Church Bodies: What characteristizes the mind of the parish is but amplified, solidified, and given enhanced authority in the larger world of the general bodies. Some years ago it became apparent to some large corporations that they had succeeded so well in fashioning the company man into symmetrical functionaries of an order that a danger was recognized. A few eccentrics were deliberately sought out, cherished, protected, and asked to give themselves to reflection uninhibited by charts.

Such sardonic maturity has not yet arisen within the churches. The fantastic rigidity, the almost awesome addiction to "channels," the specialization of concern and operation that characterize our structure have made us, in large part, prisoners of accredited mediocrity. "The wind bloweth where it listeth," but when it does a shudder of embarrassment racks the structure from top to bottom. If another J. S. Bach should occur in my church and succeed, as the first one did, in giving a new deep piety a new and adequate voice, he would have to plead his case before elected or appointed arbiters whose authority exceeds that of the consistory of Cöthen or Leipzig—and whose general cultivation is less.

The informing and edifying of the church through charismatic endowments by the Holy Spirit is not incompatable with the doctrine of One, Holy, Catholic, and Apostolic church. But it is incompatable with the church order that takes its model from the more banal children of this world. We affirm the charismatic in piety and imprison it in established structures in practice. It has actually come to pass that our churches maintain a disciplined cadre of inspirational operators. These persons are on call for whatever program the church from time to time decides to accent. They can blow any horn one hands them. If the program involves support for educational institutions they stand ready to declare across the broad reaches of the land in districts, conferences, and parishes that "the future of the church hangs upon the success of this venture in education." And when at the next general convention the scene shifts to rural missions, the same enthusiasm, now supplied with a changed terminology and directed toward a changed goal, is sent out on the road from general headquarters. One has heard this interchangeable vivacity vocalize so many and such various projects that he is reminded that the salesman is a category that can be defined quite independent of the product he sells. Whether his sample case contains hammer handles or lingerie is nothing to the point.

Self-image of the Minister: The transformation of the minister's self-image is the third force contributing to the maceration of the minister. The effects of this at the deepest levels of the man's personal life can hardly be spoken of in terms that are too grave. For this image is, strictly, not a professional or merely personal or even church-official image. It is rather an image given with the office of the ministry in and by a church in obedience to the command of the Lord of the gospel. The "Ministry of the Word and Sacraments" belongs to no man; all believers belong to it. And among these some are acknowledged as having been given a charism undergone preparation, and announced their intention to serve the gospel in this particular ministry. In the full gravity of this gift, task, and intention a man is ordained to this ministry, charged in specific terms drawn from the dominical imperative faithfully to fulfill it. The self-image of the minister is then more than a self-image; it is an image of the vocation and task of the self gathered up into a gift and a task that was before the self came to be, having a reality that transcends while it involves the whole self, and which will be bestowed upon the church by her

Lord when this particular self is no longer of the church in history.

Fragmentation has become a common term in psychology and sociology. But what has happened to the ministry is all that term suggests and reports, but more painful and accusatory because of the gravity of that public bestowing and receiving of the Lord's Ministry of Word and Sacrament. A vase can be fragmented; maceration is what a human being feels when fragmented.

It is hard for the minister to maintain a clear vision of who he is when he is so seldom doing what he ought. His self-image of a servant of the gospel has been slowly clarified, carefully matured, informed, and sensitized during years of preparation. At the time of ordination the church publicly and thankfully acknowledged a gift, a discipline, and a man's intention to assume a task.

All of this is under constant attrition in the present form of the churches. And thus it comes about that honesty in the fulfillment of the minister's central task is gradually laid aside in favor of sincerity. Sincerity is a term a man uses to enable himself to live with himself when he has uneasy questions about his honesty. There remain, however, deep down but insistent, voices and remembrances that tell the man what is going on, tell him that the exchange is not a good one. And the enthusiastic readiness of parish and church to accept, even to applaud, the shift makes the suffering of the minister the more acute.

There have been a number of studies, some widely publicized, in which attention has been called to the large number of crack-ups of various degrees of severity among the clergy. The supporting testimony is impressive. The reasons most often suggested are too much work, too long a day, too various a complex of problems and duties, too unremitting a drain on emotional and mental stores, insufficient opportunity to lift the clerical nose from the parish grindstone.

While these facts are present and powerful, the sum of them does not, I think, get to the heart of the matter. They are too obvious, too shallow; they do not designate what comes out—stumbling, embarrassed, and often gestured rather than stated—when one observes and listens with attention. From many hours spent with many former students I have learned that there is a constant fact in the variety of their confessions, overt or oblique.

These men are deeply disturbed because they have a sense of vocational guilt. This guilt is so strong, so clear, and so deeply sunk in their central self-consciousness that one knows with an immediate impatience that no diminution of hours or other re-arrangements of outer life can have decisive effect.

This sense of guilt has an observable content. A minister has been ordained to an Office; he too often ends up running an office. He was solemnly ordained to the ministry in Christ's church. Most of the men I know really want to be what they intended and prepared for. Instead they have ended up in a kind of dizzy occupational oscillation. They are aware of the truth of what Karl Barth said in one of his earliest addresses, "Our people expect us to take them more seriously than they take themselves, and they will not thank us if we do not do so." Most ministers are aware that it is a tough and delicate labor to insert the lively power of the Word of God into the rushing occupations and silent monologues of men. They recall with a sense of joy the occasions when honest work and unhurried reflection gave a strange victory to their efforts. But these occasions are infrequent, set amid great stretches of guilt-begetting busyness.

What, then, is to be done? From each of the designated constituents of the problem a different response is required. These are the professors in schools of theology, the parishes, the officials in the general bodies, the ministers themselves. Upon professors in the schools of theology there rests an immediate and pressing responsibility. Our clear perception of the demolition wrought upon our labors with students, combined with the respect accorded us by our churches, urges us out of silence and toward articulate protest. We ought to be more courageous, critical, and noisy advocates for our students, more concerned protectors of their reflective future. Our intermural grousing has now the obligation to leap over the wall and seek to make itself heard among parishes and in the offices of church officialdom. For it is there that the machinery of maceration and the pounding of program is set in motion.

It is, I think, simply not true that the parish demands of its minister that he become simply an executive officer of multiple activities. It is likely to accept, support, and be deepeningly molded by the understanding of Office and calling which is projected by its minister's actual behavior. It will come to assess as central what he, in his actual performance of his ministry and use of his time, makes central. And when this tightening and clarification of the minister's conception of his Office discloses, in the reflective depth and penetration and ordering skill of the sermon, where his heart and mind are centered, the parish will honor this pastoral obedience to "take them more seriously than they take themselves."

The officialdom of the church, and how it may be penetrated by a knowledge of the plight of the minister, presents a more difficult—because more subtle—problem. When one beholds the staff-generated devices dreamed up by boards and commissions to focus the attention of the church-in-convention assembled upon their particular programs, one wonders if the motivation is exclusively either educational or evangelical. Have these members of promotional staffs not fallen under the sovereignty of Parkinson's Law, whereby whatever *is* tends to persist, whatever *does* is driven by dynamics strange to its purpose to do more and wider and bigger? Must not each "program" outshout the

other in order to dramatize an urgency psychologically necessary
for its own sense of importance, if not priority?

One does not have to operate at the top level of the ecumenical
movement to suspect that the "nontheological factors" there exposed as powerful in church and theological history are operative
along the whole front. It is no ingratitude toward my own
family in Christendom that I take delight in the fact that there
are about one hundred million of us! And the dynamics of this
delight will not bear too much scrutiny in terms of the truth of
the gospel, the obedience to Christ, and other such properly
elevated rubrics.

We may and perhaps ought to be impatient about the world's
quip that when a man becomes a bishop he will never thereafter
eat a bad meal, read a good book, or hear the truth. But from
within the family we dare a smile. For in the very generality
that determines executive office there is a power that disengages
from the common table of parish existence, from the direct and
pathetic book of the common life, and from the moments of
sudden truth that stun and depress and exalt the minister on his
ordinary round.

Finally there is the minister himself; and in what follows I
appeal to him from the same center as has informed these lectures
on preaching. He, in his private and imperiled existence, must
fight for wholeness and depth and against erosion. By a sheer
effort of violent will he must seek to become his calling, submit
himself to be shaped in his life from the center outward. He need
not be slapped into uncorrelated fragments of function; he need
not become a weary and unstructured functionary of a vague,
busy moralism; he need not see the visions and energies and
focused loyalty of his calling run, shallowly like spilled water,
down a multitude of slopes.

Certain practical, immediate, and quite possible steps can be
taken. The temptation to improvised, catch-as-catch-can preach-

ing, for instance, can be beaten back by calculated ordering of one's study. The most profitable period in my own parish preaching came about because I did that. What I learned in seminary about Paul of Tarsus, Paul's Christology and ethics, was not sufficient either for the great subject or for the discharge of my preaching responsibility. In one memorable year I determined to bring together concentrated study and actual preaching. Surrounding myself with the best available to me from modern Pauline scholarship I literally lived with this man for six months, directed and taught by Adolph Deissman, James Stewart, Charles Harold Dodd, Robert Henry Lightfoot, J. H. Michael, and others.

Because the Philippian letter is the most direct, personal, and uncomplicated of Paul's letters I resolved to preach straight through it, informing and correcting exegesis from the Greek text by the findings and insights of historians, exegetes and theologians.

The result of this study and preaching—extending from Epiphany through Trinity Sunday—was the establishing of a love affair with this towering and impassioned "man in Christ." I came to know him with the quick and perceptive delight one has in a friend. Paul had been fused into an adoring, obedient, proclaiming and explicating totality by the fire of his new relation to God in "this Son of God who loved me . . ." And the informing of all the parts of his writing by that rooted and vivacious new being in Christ, when beheld in concentrated study, opens huge new perspectives in every single verse or section. It is not necessary to add that such an exciting discipline makes quite unnecessary the weekly scrounging for a "text."

It was a sort of added dividend that when Holy Week and Easter came around, progress through the letter had landed me precisely at Philippians 2:1-11: "And being found in human form he humbled himself and became obedient unto death, even

death on a cross. Therefore God has highly exalted him . . ."
That section, explicated on Maundy Thursday, Good Friday,
and Easter, had gained a momentum from the twelve preceding
sermons on chapters 1 and 2 that was both powerful and full
for the preacher and for the people.

The foregoing is an illustration, it is not a prescription. Each
man must order his life from the inside, and each must order it
according to the requirements of interest, nature, and parish
situation. But order it he must.

Appendix

THE SHAPE OF THE CHURCH'S RESPONSE IN WORSHIP[1]

THE PROBLEM: A DESCRIPTION

Faith and Order created a Commission on Worship in acknowledgment of a fact. The fact is that the way Christian people worship is declarative of what they believe. This declaration may well be made in worship at a depth and with a fullness seldom attained in credal propositions.

Early in Faith and Order inquiries it became apparent that formal comparative examination of the confessional and other utterances of the churches was not adequate for a responsible understanding either of what these churches affirmed in common or asserted in difference. There is a worship of the one God by his one people; that is why a Commission on Worship is possible and necessary. And there is a wild and bewildering variety in ways of worship by this one people: that is why the work of this commission is difficult.

It is not necessary to go into great detail concerning the present constitution of the commission as reorganized following the second assembly of the World Council of Churches at Evanston.

[1] Originally presented as a report to the North American Faith and Order Conference at Oberlin, Ohio, in September, 1957.

It is enough for our present purpose to remember that three commissions in widely separated and quite different areas were established: one in Europe, one in East Asia, one in North America.
While some preliminary correspondence has been carried on
with the European commission, and while all of us in the area-
commission are aware of and grateful for the vigorous and pro-
ductive work of the East Asian group—this is a discussion of
matters which have arisen in the two meetings which have been
held under my chairmanship in North America.

One cannot get very far in constructive thought about a problem until the nature of the problem has been clearly exposed. Our
work of exposure is by no means complete, but certain aspects
are clear enough that I can point them out in the confidence that
any concerned listener will recognize what I am talking about.

The term "worship" presents a problem. At the second meet-
ing of our commission Professor Leonard Trinterud with characteristic bluntness and clarity excised this particular problem
in these words: "Our English word 'worship' misstates the whole
content and significance of that which in the New Testament is
called 'the service of God,' i.e., *leiturgia, latria, diakonia,* and
their respective related terms.

"In the New Testament these terms refer normatively to
'serving God,' 'doing the will of God,' in a great variety of ways
most of which are without cultic significance or form, and which
refer principally to that which is done for and among men—not
to something done to or for God in a sanctuary. The New
Testament knows nothing of a *leiturgia, latria, diakonia* which is
localized in an edifice, or to fixed times of occurrence. These
terms refer to the whole round of the Christians' ordinary life as
people."

Professor Trinterud made his second point as follows: "Acts
such as prayer, thanksgiving, breaking of bread, are regarded in
the New Testament as but an aspect of the 'service of God,' and

that not the controlling or central aspect. That which in the New Testament *is* central and controlling in the 'service of God,' is the presence of Christ, the Head of the church, in the Holy Spirit given to the church. The living Christ, thus present, directs, guides, builds up the church, and thus it 'serves God.' Our ideas of worship are too often rooted in the situation of the people of God before the Resurrection and Pentecost. There, indeed, priests, strictly so-called, performed cultic acts, in properly consecrated sanctuaries, acts addressed to God on behalf of the people. But the new aeon comes when the promise of God has been fulfilled, when the redeeming work of God has been done in Christ, and when the Holy Spirit has been given to all believers. God's people are now related to him in a new and living way previously only promised. So, also, God is now present among his people, by the Holy Spirit, a manner of presence which previously was but a promise.

"We cannot discuss 'worship' as though we were still in the old aeon, on the other side of Pentecost and the Resurrection."

One can disagree with a great deal of what Professor Trinterud says, but such disagreement has little to do with the size or importance of the problem thus explicated. Our commission has been sufficiently impressed to agree upon the following:

a. A thoroughgoing biblical inquiry into the relation between the "service of God" and what we have come to call the "service of worship" by the congregation of believers assembled in a specific place has got to be undertaken. The enormous exegetical ferment which has been engendered by recent decades of brilliant and notion-cracking biblical studies makes it quite impossible to derive schematically neat ideas about worship from the New Testament community. Some old certainties have been made untenable, and a confusing and exciting richness of life has been exposed.

b. The interdependence of the work of the Commission on Worship and the Commission on Christ and the Church is transparently clear. Just as the doctrine of the church was at Lund shifted to a position under the doctrine of Christ, so also, we think, the inquiry into worship must be illuminated from the same center.

A corollary of these convictions has shaped our commission's understanding of its task—and it may be expressed here as a kind of an aside. If any of us came to this study as liturgiologists, or were under the impression that by becoming such we could best advance our work, we have long since laid such notions aside. There is a place and a useful function to be served by such inquiries, but none of us is disposed to interpret our directive in such terms. Descriptive and analytical inquiries into ways of worship must follow a clear understanding of the nature and scope and meaning of worship. If liturgical considerations precede such studies, the deeper question is either dismissed or too quickly set in doctrinaire terms.

c. Inquiry into the nature of Christian worship of God has, particularly in North America, got to operate in a sphere of discourse already occupied. The name of the occupant, in very many of our congregations, is the psychology of worship. This strange roomer got into and established himself in the living room of church practice in roughly the following way: that people do worship God is an observable fact; and every fact is permeable to psychological inquiry. Psychology does not operate from hand to mouth; it has either open or unavowed presuppositions about the structure and dynamics of the psyche. If, then, in worship people are in some way or other in search of a relationship to the Ineffable there must be ways which lubricate and ways which hinder this search. The human animal is influenced by setting, accompaniment, symbols, silence, the gravity of statement and response, the solidarity-producing impact of solemn music, etc.

So it has happened that experts in worship have arisen among us. All assume that the purpose of public worship is to create a mood; and he is the next admirable as the leader of worship who has mastered finesse in the mood-setting devices made available by the application of psychological categories. Thence has flowed that considerable and melancholy river of counsel whereby one may learn how to organize an assault upon the cognitive and critical faculties of the mind, how to anesthetize into easy seduction the nonverbalized but dependable anxieties that roam about in the solitary and collective unconscious, and how to conduct a brain-washing under the presumed banner of the Holy Ghost.

That this is what worship means in thousands of congregations is certainly true; it is equally true that the scriptures know nothing about such ideas. When we are enjoined to be still and know that God is God, the presupposition is not that stillness is good and speech is bad—but rather that God is *prior* to man and all God-man relationships are out of joint if that is not acknowledged.

d. The third problem of which we have become acutely aware is a big and general problem; and I cannot advance toward a description of it until I shove out of the way an unhappy term which is well on the way to ecumenical canonization. It is a nontheological factor! Which is saying an unintelligible thing. For there are no nontheological factors in human existence. To suppose that there are is to misunderstand both the scope and intention of Christian theology and the actualities of human thought and feeling.

This tough third problem then can best be delineated by starting with a proposition: that language is the primary creation and carrier of culture, and it follows the career of man's culture with absolute seriousness. Language, that is to say, in the structure, scope, and content of it, is an obedient transcript of what a people understands itself and its world to be like. When that world-understanding is mono-dimensional, language loses its opulence. When that world-meaning becomes a plane without extension or depth, language becomes designative and thin.

I cannot here investigate why language in our time has become flat, nonallusive, and impoverished, but simply to observe that it *has* and ask what this means for our churches as they seek to recover ways of worship which shall be more adequate to the object of worship, and more fully reflective of the long history of the people of God in their life of worship.

It is strange that this problem, so widely acknowledged and so profoundly disturbing outside the churches, has, so far as I know, not been systematically discussed among us. This is the more strange because the more deeply a concern is loaded with history, the past, things accomplished long ago, the more a church understands herself as a "pilgrim people of God"—that is, called, continuous, on the way, starting with a constitutive deed and living out her life in a hope which is both a given and an awaited consummation—the more clearly the church understands *that*, the more embarrassing her problem with a flat and impoverished language. Just as our Christology becomes richer, our ecclesiology more organic, our anthropology deeper—our common language, the cultural instrument that must do the work of acknowledgment, praise, and interpretation, is shrinking in obedience to a diminished realm of meaning.

The gravity of rhythmic speech is the mark of a culture that carries its past livingly in its present experience. Rhythmic speech is the outward and visible sign of rootedness. Every society has had its rhetoric of remembrance. "Come now, let us bring our reasoning to a close, saith the Lord. . . . Israel doth not know, my people doth not consider. . . . I am the Lord thy God that brought thee out of that great and terrible wilderness. . . . I have called thee by thy name, thou art mine."

In the scriptures each moment is heavy with all past moments, for the God of the moment is the creator of the continuity. The old prayers of the church understood this so well and felt it so deeply that every one of them jumps into the moments' petitions after a running start in the eventful history of the people of God. "O God, who didst teach the hearts of Thy faithful people by sending to them the light of Thy Holy Spirit: Grant us by the same Spirit to have a right judgment in all things, and evermore to rejoice in His holy comfort. . . ." This is great rhetoric because it roots the life of the moment in the grace of the past; it evokes a response in depth because it is not only a report, but a reverberation. It is an expectant episode in a people's life because it is a note in ancient and continuing music. It is as big as the heart because it is as old as the people of God.

How many times, in reading the liturgy for the Holy Communion, I have felt both exultation and despair at the moment of the Sanctus: "Therefore with Angels and Archangels, and with all the company of heaven, we laud and magnify Thy glorious Name; evermore praising Thee, and saying: Holy, Holy, Holy, Lord God of Saboath . . ." Exalted because, in this language, this place and time and company of momentary lives are interpreted and blessed within the scope of an eternal action of God, released from the tyranny of death and what Dylan Thomas has so movingly alluded to when he laments that

> *. . . time in all its tuneless turning allows*
> *So few, and such morning songs . . .*

But also in despair for to the flattened speech of our time angels and archangels are rather ridiculous symbols—material, so to speak, nonfissionable by contemporary definition of fact.

Strange things nevertheless are happening in the present practice of language. Just when one is sodden with despair over the possibility of making alive the massive biblical symbol of *fire*, for instance—

> *Come Holy Ghost, our souls inspire*
> *And lighten with celestial fire;*

just then man does such things with language as to reinvest this symbol with meanings and dreamed of meanings of terrible force. The immediate referent of *fire* in 1957 is not the celestial fire of God's descending and recreating ardor—but a monstrous shape like a death-dealing mushroom. And out of this unimaginable hell a man envisions again an unbelievable grace, and writes in language which wildly fuses destroying atom bombs and the descending Holy Ghost:

> The dove descending breaks the air
> With flame of incandescent terror
> Of which the tongues declare
> The one discharge from sin and error
> The only hope, or else despair
> Lies in the choice of pyre or pyre
> To be redeemed from fire by fire.

T. S. ELIOT

Such speech judges one's tepid unbelief in the power of the Holy Spirit of God, reminds us that the aggressive and ingenious love that can make the stones cry out can penetrate positivistic language too, and betimes torment its flatness into a kind of "negative" praise.

It is therefore proper to our study of worship to inquire what this revolution in language means for the public worship in our churches; to ask whether perhaps it is not a task of contemporary obedience and praise to find fresh forms of statement whereby intelligibly to set forth ancient facts and encounters. It may well be that we are entering upon a period in the church's life wherein men's minds must be shocked open to entertain the suspicion that there are realms of meaning, promise, and judgment which ensconce God's incarnated action for their vague disquietudes.

THE PROBLEM:

CONSTRUCTIVE ANALYSIS

There has never been a church which has not declared its faith and order to be continuous with the apostolic tradition. Some churches have affirmed this explicitly in their confessions or other basic writings; others have unfolded their life, eschewing confessional statements, but claiming to celebrate this tradition in teaching, order, and piety.

This fact opens up a double way to make an entrance into the constructive part of our task. One way is to mobilize all resources for an ever-fresh encounter with the actual content of the apostolic tradition and judge the public worship in our churches according to their congruity with its announcement, promise, and demand. This does not of course assume that there *are*, in the apostolic tradition, clear and commanding directives concerning the form and content of public worship; it affirms, rather, that ways of worship which ignore or distort the liberating message of God's Christly action must be corrected from that central action.

The other way is to examine the phenomena of public worship as carried on by the various churches; peer behind the accents and selections which have actually modified all of them; get beyond the cultural deposits in the form of language, music, gesture, etc., which cling to all of them; and ask if there is *morphology* of the response of the people of God.

The hope is that there may emerge among us, as we inquire

into these matters, a way of thinking about worship which will liberate us from our placid captivity within our separate traditions. We are asking if there is a unity in the entire worshiping career of the responding faithful people of God, whence this unity comes, and what is its essential content.

The earliest Christian communities to whose life we have literary access apparently believed there was such a unity. This consensus concerning the apostolic tradition is the more remarkable in view of the broad and detailed New Testament studies which have elaborated the rich and sometimes confusing variety out of which the voice of this consensus speaks. Before the Gospels, in the form we now know them, existed, the church was giving voice to the general shape and content of what it believed God had accomplished in Christ—which action called it into being, sustained and enabled its life, and furnished it with both task and power. God, it was affirmed, had engaged himself in a personal, incarnate action with man's estranged and captive predicament, had recapitulated in Jesus Christ the entire life of Adam (his created but now estranged human family), had involved himself with every tragedy, limitation, desolation, and even the death of man.

This God-initiated, ingressive penetration of human life is the substance of those records which are the Four Gospels. Each, to be sure, has its own character; each has sources unknown to or unused by the others; and each is shaped in accent and use of materials by circumstances known to us to some degree.

But the morphology of the action of God in Christ is alike in all. Its shape is an inverted parabola. The starting point is the appearance of One who asserted that he came to announce and inaugurate the kingly rule of God in such a way as to actualize the hopes of the people of God, make effective the liberating promise and power of God, establish men—by his life and teaching and deeds—in a new relationship to God and to one another.

This lived-out action had a shape which was that of a descending curve which went down, into, through, and under every broken God-relationship, and was apparently destroyed at the nadir of its career on Good Friday.

The Gospels, however, are resurrection documents. They declare that God, who is alive, is not stopped in his purpose by the assault of death, but rather carried his action through. His Word, Jesus Christ, is victorious over death, lives, reigns, is the second Adam, the Head of a new body—the church. The old creed of the church follows episodically the precise pattern of the parabola of the grace of God—born, suffered, died, arose, ascended, reigns with the Father.

This declaration is the core of the apostolic tradition. We confront it repeatedly in the Acts of the Apostles and in that body of correspondence available to us in the letters of Paul. Especially clarifying and impressive is the way Paul, caught in a polemical situation, again and again appeals to this tradition. In such situations the apostle reaches, as it were, back of himself and back of his hearers, gets hold of the given core of what commands him and them, and strides into the point at issue as from a secure beachhead. That these moments occur in the course of the rough and tumble of his pastoral career and not, as a rule, as calculated links in a chain of argument makes them the more startling. Paul did not, apparently, so schematize his words to the Philippians as to lead up to the great words in chapter 2, verses 5-11. He is simply appealing to this community—which was in a fix—to be "like-minded" in the "fellowship of the Spirit."

This fellowship involves a "lowliness of mind." And whence is that? Where shall one behold it, whence receive it? Led on then by the questions his own counsel has generated the apostle cannot stop short of sinking the present life of the Philippian community in the entire deed of God in Jesus Christ. So, almost accidentally, does the all-shaping apostolic core reveal its massive shape behind an occasional pastoral message. This passage is not Christology in order to Christology; it is Christology in order to ethics. And the more persuasive for that reason.

In the letter to the Romans Paul is called upon to confront a flippant and almost blasphemous non sequitur—a situation not unknown to any preacher or teacher today. If grace abounds more abundantly where sin abounds in force, then one is in the amazing situation of eating and having his cake at the same time! Against such total incomprehension of his message Paul wheels up the heavy artillery of the apostolic tradition.

The shape of the deed of God, he declares, engenders a *total* human life in organic congruity with itself; and to be a Christian is to have one's life in *its* shape determined by the shape of what God has done. Therefore, says Paul, what happened to Christ is the God-given, redemptive pattern of our lives. "Know ye not that so many of us as were baptized into Jesus Christ were baptized into his death? Therefore we are buried with him by baptism into death: that like as Christ was raised up from the dead by the glory of the Father, even so we also should walk in newness of life."

As then, the morphology of grace in the life, death, resurrection, and exaltation of Jesus Christ imparts to and creates in the believer its own shape—so worship is the name proper to the celebration of this new being in Christ by his body, the church. Such a celebration has a scope broad enough to include all the New Testament means by *leitorgia, latria, diakonia* (the service of God), and has enough specific concreteness to be verbalized in the liturgical life of the church where it is assembled in public worship. Any definition of worship less rich than this comes under the judgment of such an admonition as Paul's in the twelfth chapter of Romans. "I appeal to you therefore, brethren, by the mercies of God, to present your bodies as a living sacrifice, holy and acceptable to God, which is your spiritual worship."

As then we perceive the bare elements of the apostolic message, and observe how this shape, re-enacted within the behavior by the power of the Holy Spirit, constituted Christian life in the fellowship of the community, do we not also, perhaps, find a pattern for Christian worship? Is there not here a given substance and morphology of response which presses upon all of us, calls all of us to attend, acknowledge, and celebrate? If that is so, then we are given a starting place where, from within our various churches, we ask after what is constitutive of and proper to the content of truly catholic worship.

Every tradition in Christian worship acknowledges that it does indeed stand under this given substance of the gospel. This is overtly so among the churches which cherish liturgical patterns centuries old; it is covertly so among churches whose public worship is improvised, *ad hoc*, and so free as to make the term "tradition" strange. The directive of the churches represented in Faith and Order—that a study of worship be pursued over a number of years—indicates a recognition that there is a *giveness* to Christian worship, and that the common degradation of worship into gimmicks for religious mood-engendering is a kind of impoverishment, a failure, a positive disobedience hiding behind the face of individualism, spontaneity, freedom.

Remembering then the apostolic tradition, and having in mind the huge spectrum of forms of public worship within the churches—from nonliturgical churches on one side to Eastern Orthodoxy on the other—there is none that does not acknowledge in public worship the following five elements: recollection, thanksgiving, participation, proclamation, expectation.

Recollection. A congregation of believers assembled for the public worship of God knows that it did not come into existence at that moment, knows that it is not alone, knows that what is happening is happening because something *has* happened from

God's side. What is announced is continuous with what has been announced since the Resurrection.

And therefore all sequences of public worship include, whether in formal liturgical or informal ways, powerful elements of recollection. Mighty deeds have been done, a huge liberation has taken place, an event called Jesus Christ was, is, and is here—and everything that takes place presupposes that. "In the name of the Father, and of the Son, and of the Holy Ghost . . . In the beginning was the Word, and the Word was with God, and the Word was God . . . In many and various ways God spoke of old to our fathers by the prophets; but in these last days he has spoken to us by a love . . . In all these things we are more than conquerors through him that loved us . . ."

Celebration begins with recollection.

Recollection engenders *thanksgiving*. The content of what is recalled in worship is not a cluster of episodes spiritually elevated above, but essentially continuous with, the structures of human history. These remembered deeds of creation, care, deliverance, and renewal are rather the recital of faith in which is perceived within the structure of history the ultimate redemption of man. Exodus is an occurrence, and a power-bearing symbol; Incarnation is an occurrence, and the radical mercy of God whereby he did and does what needs doing in the sin and death determined house of man's existence. As then ". . . although they know God they did not honor him as God or give thanks to him"; nevertheless, ". . . when the time had fully come God sent forth his Son, born of a woman, born under the law, to redeem those who were under the law, so that we might receive adoption as sons."

Therefore, "Thanks be to God for his inexpressible gift." "And all the angels stood 'round the throne, . . . and they fell on their faces and worshiped God, saying, Amen! Blessing and glory and wisdom and thanksgiving and honor and power and might be to our God for ever and ever! Amen."

The church's thankful recollection of God's deed of redemption is at the same time a *participation*. Hearing, repentance, acceptance of mercy, forgiveness of sins—these are all the work of God whereby man receives no less than a "new-being in Christ." Rich and various are the New Testament images in which this new-being is promised and, given in faith, celebrated. Men are *before* Christ, who beholds them; *under* Christ, who judges them; for or against Christ, who addresses them. But the thrust and destiny of this holy encounter is that they may be *in* Christ! The language of participation dominates the New Testament speech about the fullness of the Christ relationship. "I am the vine; you are the branches." "If any man be in Christ he is a new creation, old things have passed away." "I live, yet not I, but Christ lives in me . . . the life which I now live I live by this Son of God who loved me . . ." "For you have died, and your life is hid with Christ in God."

Christian worship is *proclamation*. The substance of what is proclaimed is the same as what is recollected, the same as is now acknowledged by the congregation in thanksgiving as God's salvatory and present power, the same as is offered and received in participation of the members in the Head of the church. Worship not only includes proclamation of the gospel of salvation, it *is* proclamation.

Every service of public worship is a banner of life flying among the banners of mortality. Every assembly of believers in the name of Christ is a proclamation of the *Regnum Dei* by subjects and sons who have been liberated and now live in the *Regnum Christi*. The celebration of the Supper of the Lord is indeed recollection, Eucharist, the seal of forgiveness of sins, and the gift and nurturing of life in the Lord of the feast. But it is something more: something immediate and poignant in the embattled "little flocks" of the first century, known again in our day by millions in shattered and cut-off lives in cells, rubble, behind wire, and behind curtains.

It is the proclamation of engrafted membership in a kingdom not born of history, and therefore not at the mercy of history's demonic tyrannies. The somber chalice has in our day again become a defiant sign uplifted, the believer's "toast of terrible joy." "As often as you eat this bread and drink this cup, you proclaim the Lord's death until he comes."

But all of this recollection, thanksgiving, participation, and proclamation is the worship, or true service of God, in the body within the theater of this world; a response and a song of praise by the *pilgrim* people of God. And for that reason Christian worship is always *expectation*. This expectation is not an element in a richer context, it is rather the pervading mood of the whole of Christian worship. If I had not been *given* an immeasurable gift I could not expect at all; if this gift were consummated within the conditions of human existence I could not expect, either.

The last word of the New Testament is a dramatic condensation of this "not yet—yet even now." The Apocalypse of St. John concludes, "Amen. Come, Lord Jesus!" The Amen leans backward toward the mighty salvatory deeds of God, affirms that the church, the Body of Christ, is held in God's hand against the powers of hell. The "Come, Lord Jesus" leans forward toward the consummation of "the fullness of him who fills all in all."

The Christian life is a life drawn taut between the Amen and the Come. This tautness has its suffering, its waiting, and its peculiar service to the world. And inasmuch as Christian worship has been the strange music of these taut and joyous lives in history, a deep study of worship points a steady finger to the nature of the unity we seek.

Date Due